Da

Fir

ألعاب نارية

Translated by Clem Naylor

Bloomsbury Methuen Drama
An imprint of Bloomsbury Publishing Plc

B L O O M S B U R Y
LONDON · NEW DELHI · NEW YORK · SYDNEY

Bloomsbury Methuen Drama

An imprint of Bloomsbury Publishing Plc

Imprint previously known as Methuen Drama

50 Bedford Square	1385 Broadway
London	New York
WC1B 3DP	NY 10018
UK	USA

www.bloomsbury.com

**BLOOMSBURY, METHUEN DRAMA and the Diana
logo are trademarks of Bloomsbury Publishing Plc**

British Library Cataloguing-in-Publication Data
A catalogue record for this book is available from the British Library.

ISBN PB: 978-1-4742-4450-3
ePub: 978-1-4742-4452-7
ePDF: 978-1-4742-4451-0

Library of Congress Cataloging-in-Publication Data
A catalog record for this book is available from the Library of Congress.

Typeset by Mark Heslington Ltd, Scarborough, North Yorkshire

THE ROYAL COURT
THEATRE PRESENTS

By Dalia Taha
Translated by Clem Naylor

FIREWORKS

ألعاب نارية

Fireworks was first performed at
the Royal Court Jerwood Theatre
Upstairs, Sloane Square, on
Thursday 12 February 2015.

Fireworks is presented as part of International Playwrights: A Genesis
Foundation Project, with additional support from the British Council and
the A.M. Qattan Foundation.

FIREWORKS ألعاب نارية
BY DALIA TAHA
Translated by CLEM NAYLOR

CAST (in alphabetical order)

Khalid **Saleh Bakri**
Ahmad **Nabil Elouahabi**
Khalil **Yusuf Hofri**
Khalil **George Karageorgis**
Samar **Shereen Martin**
Lubna **Eden Nathenson**
Lubna **Shakira Riddell-Morales**
Nahla **Sirine Saba**

Director **Richard Twyman**
Designer **Lizzie Clachan**
Lighting Designer **Natasha Chivers**
Composer **Benedict Taylor**
Sound Designer **George Dennis**
Voice & Dialect Coach **Zabarjad Salam**
Assistant Director **Diyan Zora**
International Director **Elyse Dodgson**
International Administrator **Callum Smith**
Casting Director **Louis Hammond**
Production Manager **Tariq Rifaat**
Costume Supervisor **Lydia Crimp**
Chaperones **Justin Kielty, Tanya Shields**
Stage Managers **Julia Slienger, Sophia Dalton**
Stage Management Work Placement **Rachel Hendry**
Set constructed by **Ridiculous Solutions**

The Royal Court wish to thank the following for their help with this production:
Al Harah theatre, Beit Jala, Caryl Churchill, Cas & Philip Donald.

FIREWORKS ألعاب نارية
THE COMPANY

Dalia Taha (Writer)

Theatre includes: **Keffiyeh (Made in China) (Flemish Royal/A.M. Qattan Foundation).**

Dalia is a Palestinian poet and playwright. She participated in the Royal Court International Residency in 2013 where she began to work on Fireworks. She is currently pursuing an MFA in Playwriting at Brown University and has published two collections of poetry and one novel.

Saleh Bakri (Khalid)

Theatre includes: **Junoon (Craziness), Forget Herostratus (Almidan, Haifa); Point of You (Dramatikkens Hus, Oslo/Alrowah, Jerusalem).**

Film includes: **The Time That Remains, Salt of This Sea, Salvo, When I Saw You, The Source, The Band's Visit.**

Lizzie Clachan (Designer)

For the Royal Court: **Adler & Gibb, Gastronauts, Jumpy, Wastwater, Our Private Life, Aunt Dan & Lemon, The Girlfriend Experience (& Drum Theatre, Plymouth), On Insomnia & Midnight (& Festival Internacional Cervantino, Guanajuato/Centro Cultural Helénico, Mexico City), Shoot/Get Treasure/Repeat (& National/Out of Joint/Paines Plough), Woman & Scarecrow (& RSC), Ladybird.**

Other theatre includes: **Treasure Island, Edward II, Port, A Woman Killed with Kindness (National); The Forbidden Zone (Salzburg/Berlin); All My Sons (Regent's Park Open Air); A Sorrow Beyond Dreams (Burgtheater, Vienna); A Season in the Congo, The Soldier's Fortune (Young Vic); Longing, The Trial of Ubu, Tiger Country (Hampstead); Rings of Saturn (Shauspiel, Cologne); Crave/Illusions (ATC); Happy Days (Crucible, Sheffield); Far Away (Bristol Old Vic); Treasure Island (West End); The Architects, Money, Tropicana, Amato Saltone, Ether Frolics, Dance Bear Dance, The Ballad of Bobby François, The Tennis Show (Shunt); Contains Violence, Absolute Beginners (Lyric, Hammersmith); Julie, Gobbo (National Theatre of Scotland); Factory Girls (Arcola); I'll Be the Devil, Days of Significance, The American Pilot (RSC).**

Opera includes: **Le Vin Herbé (Staatstoper, Berlin); Bliss (Staatsoper, Hamburg).**

Awards include: **UK Theatre Award for Best Design (Happy Days – with Natasha Chivers).**

Lizzie co-founded Shunt in 1998 and is an Artistic Director of the company.

Natasha Chivers (Lighting Designer)

For the Royal Court: **Adler & Gibb, The Mistress Contract, Gastronauts, The Djinns of Eidgah, That Face (& West End).**

Other theatre includes: **Juno & The Paycock (Bristol Old Vic/Liverpool Playhouse); 1984 (Headlong/Almeida/West End); Macbeth (National Theatre of Scotland/ Broadway); The Green Snake (National Theatre of China); Praxis Makes Perfect (Neon Neon/National Theatre Wales); The Radicalisation of Bradley Manning (National Theatre Wales); 27, The Wheel, Home: Glasgow, Mary Stuart, The House of Bernard Alba, Empty/The Miracle Man (National Theatre of Scotland); Boeing Boeing, One Monkey Don't Stop No Show, The Village Bike, Happy Days (Crucible, Sheffield); And the Horse You Rode in On (Told By An Idiot); Statement of Regret (National); Sunday in the Park with George (West End); The Wolves in the Walls (National Theatre of Scotland/ Improbable); Othello, Dirty Wonderland, Pool (No Water), Tiny Dynamite, Peepshow, Hymns, Sell-Out (Frantic Assembly).**

Dance includes: **The Talent – Ballet Boyz (Linbury); Motor Show (LIFT/Brighton Festival); Electric Hotel (Sadler's Wells/ Fuel); Electric Counterpoint (ROH); God's Garden (Arthur Pita/ROH Linbury/tour); Scattered, Broken (Motionhouse/tour/ Queen Elizabeth Hall); Run!, Renaissance (Greenwich & Docklands International Festival); Beyond Belief (Legs on the Wall/ Carriageworks, Sydney); Encore (Sadler's Wells); The Ballet Boyz (Royal Festival Hall).**

Awards include: **Olivier Award for Best Lighting Design (Sunday in the Park with George); UK Theatre Award for Best Design (Happy Days) (with Lizzie Clachan); Theatre Critics of Wales Award for Best Lighting Design (Praxis Makes Perfect).**

George Dennis (Sound Designer)

For the Royal Court: **Liberian Girl.**

Other theatre includes: **Beautiful Thing (West End/UK tour); Visitors (Bush); The Edge** of Our Bodies, Dances of Death (Gate); Regeneration (Royal & Derngate/UK tour); Mametz (National Theatre Wales); peddling (59E59, New York/HighTide Festival); Moth (Bush/HighTide Festival); Minotaur (Polka/Clwyd Theatr Cymru); Spring Awakening (Headlong); The Island (Young Vic); Love Your Soldiers (Crucible Studio, Sheffield); The Last Yankee (Print Room); Thark (Park); Hello/Goodbye (Hampstead); Liar Liar (Unicorn); Good Grief (Theatre Royal, Bath/UK tour); The Seven Year Itch (Salisbury Playhouse); When Did You Last See My Mother? (Trafalgar Studios); The Seagull, The Only True History of Lizzie Finn (Southwark); A Life, Foxfinder (Finborough); The Living Room (Jermyn Street).

Nabil Elouahabi (Ahmad)

Theatre includes: **The Nightmares of Carlos Fuentes (Arcola); Love Your Soldiers (Crucible, Sheffield); The Great Game – Afghanistan (Tricycle/US tour); Crossing Jerusalem (Tricycle); Rest upon the Wind (Middle East tour); Sparkleshark (UK tour); East is East (Oldham Coliseum); Wish (OvalHouse).**

Television includes: **Crime, 24, Top Boy, Maddogs, Strikeback, Generation Kill, The Path to 9/11, EastEnders, Only Fools & Horses.**

Film includes: **Hyena Road, Reign of the General, Zero Dark Thirty, Towerblock, Junkhearts, Blitz, Journey to Mecca, The Boat People, Charlie Wilson's War, Code 46, In This World, Ali G indahouse, The Sum of all Fears.**

Yusuf Hofri (Khalil)

Theatre includes: **Thriller Live (West End).**

Film includes: **Grimsby.**

George Karageorgis (Khalil)

This is George's professional stage debut.

Shereen Martin (Samar)

Theatre includes: **Tonight at 8:30 (ETT); Ciphers (Out of Joint/Bush/Exeter Northcott); The Only True History of Lizzie Finn (Southwark); The Bomb, The Great Game (Tricycle); The Black Album, The Hour We Knew Nothing of Each Other (National); Fallujah (Old Truman Brewery); The Bachae (Abbey, Dublin); Tejas Verdes (Gate); Twelfth Night (Albery); The Turn of the Screw (Wolsey); Measure for Measure, Richard III, Titus Andronicus (RSC); Romeo & Juliet (Liverpool Playhouse).**

Television includes: **A Mother's Son, Lewis, Doctors, EastEnders, The Bill, Holby City, The Last Detective.**

Film includes: **Britz.**

Eden Nathenson (Lubna)

Theatre includes: **Jonah Man Jazz (St James).**

Television includes: **Army Kids.**

Film includes: **Dolls Can't Cry, Christmas Time, Radio Radio, Santa Claus is Dead.**

Clem Naylor (Translator)

Translations for the Royal Court: **Online, Withdrawal, Keffiyeh (Made in China) (& Mosaic Rooms).**

Other translations include: **A Chance Encounter (Theatre Uncut/Young Vic).**

Clem got his BA in Arabic and French in 2009 and his MSt in Modern Middle Eastern Studies in 2010, both from Oxford University. He has been translating Arabic plays since 2007, when he returned from a year in Damascus.

Shakira Riddell-Morales (Lubna)

Theatre includes: **Les Misérables (West End).**

Television includes: **Basil & Barney's Swap Shop, Small Potatoes.**

Sirine Saba (Nahla)

Theatre includes: **Next Fall (Southwark); Antony & Cleopatra, Holy Warriors, (Globe); The Keepers of Infinite Space (The Park); The Winter's Tale, The Taming of the Shrew, A Midsummer Night's Dream, Twelfth Night, HMS Pinafore (Regent's Park Open Air); The Fear of Breathing (Finborough); Scorched (Old Vic); Nation, Sparkleshark (National); Testing the Echo (Out of Joint/Tricycle); Baghdad Wedding (Soho); Beauty & the Beast, Midnight's Children, Pericles, The Tempest, The Winter's Tale, Tales from Ovid, A Midsummer Night's Dream, A Warwickshire Testimony (RSC); House & Garden (Royal & Derngate).**

Television includes: **Doctors, I Am Slave, Silent Witness, Footballer's Wives, The Bill, Prometheus.**

Film includes: **Exhibition, Maestro, Revolution.**

Radio includes: **Morning, The Brick, The Outsider, The Insider, The Reluctant Spy, The Deportation Room, In the Van, Marley Was Dead, My Daughter the Racist, The Smell of Fish, The Casper Logue Affair, A Dish of Pomegranates, The Porter &**

the Three Ladies, English in Afghanistan, The Locust & the Bird, Beirut Days, The Waves, The Night of the Mirage, Baghdad Wedding, Love & Loss.

Zabarjad Salam (Voice & Dialect Coach)

For the Royal Court: **Liberian Girl, Khandan (Family) (& Birmingham Rep), The Djinns of Eidgah, Death Tax, NSFW.**

Other theatre includes: **Behind the Beautiful Forevers, The Veil, 13, The Comedy of Errors, The Animals and Children Took to the Streets, Travelling Light, Collaborators, The Last of the Haussmans, Timon of Athens, This House (National); My Night with Reg (Donmar); Saturday Night Fever, Speed the Plow, Hayfever, Who's Afraid of Virginia Woolf? (Theatre Royal, Bath); Othello (Frantic Assembly); We Are Proud to Present (Bush); Other Desert Cities (Old Vic); Urinetown (St James/West End); Once a Catholic (Tricycle); The Island, Sizwe Bansi is Dead (Young Vic); Matilda, The Commitments, Let It Be (West End); The Empress, Julius Caesar, The Winter's Tale, Much Ado About Nothing (RSC); Goodnight Mr Tom (Chichester Festival); The Emperor Self (Arcola); Zaide (Sadler's Wells/UK tour).**

Television includes: **Being Eileen, Blandings, Cucumber, Indian Summers, Cilla.**

Film includes: **Tulip Fever.**

Benedict Taylor (Composer)

For the Royal Court: **The Djinns of Eidgah.**

Film includes: **Maunraag, The Bright Day, Killa, Ship of Theseus, Harud, That Girl in Yellow Boots, Waves of Power, Citizen Soldiers, Butoh.**

Awards include: **Crystal Bear & International Jury Award – Berlinale (Killa); TIFF Transylvania Trophy (Ship of Theseus); BFI Jury Special Mention, HKIFF Signis Award, London Critics Circle: Selection Centenary '15 Films That Changed My Life' (Ship of Theseus); New York SAIFF Grand Jury Award (The Bright Day).**

Richard Twyman (Director)

For the Royal Court: **The Djinns of Eidgah; PIIGS (Open Court).**

Other theatre includes: **Henry IV Pt II (RSC); Ditch (Old Vic Tunnels/HighTide); Dr Marigold & Mr Chops (Theatre Royal, Bath & UK tour); Sixty-Six Books (Bush); Give Me Your Hand (Irish Rep, New York).**

Awards include: **Olivier Awards for Best Company Performance & Best Revival, Evening Standard Editor's Choice Award (Henry IV Pt II, The Histories Cycle).**

Richard is International Associate at the Royal Court Theatre.

Diyan Zora (Assistant Director)

As Assistant Director, for the Royal Court: **The Wolf from the Door.**

As Director, theatre includes: **Gather Ye Rosebuds (Nightingale, Brighton/503); Twelfth Night (Cockpit); Othello (Barons Court).**

As Assistant Director, theatre includes: **The Nightmares of Carlos Fuentes (Arcola); My Name Is (Arcola/UK tour); Don Juan (Cockpit).**

Feb – Jun 2015

JERWOOD THEATRE DOWNSTAIRS

Until 21 Mar
How To Hold Your Breath
by Zinnie Harris

An epic look at the true cost of principles and how we live now.

7 Apr – 31 May
Roald Dahl's
The Twits
adapted by Enda Walsh

Mischievously adapted from one of the world's most loved books, Enda Walsh turns THE TWITS upside down.

PECKHAM AND TOTTENHAM

Until 14 Feb
Liberian Girl
by Diana Nneka Atuona

This Alfred Fagon award-winning play tells one teenage girl's story of survival during the Liberian Civil War.

3–7 Feb, CLF Theatre, Bussey Building, Peckham.

10–14 Feb, Bernie Grant Arts Centre, Tottenham.

WEST END

Until 25 Apr
The Nether
by Jennifer Haley

★★★★★
"Mind-bending ... Ingenious"
The Times

Duke of York's Theatre.

Presented by Sonia Friedman Productions and Scott M Delman in association with Tulchin Bartner productions, Lee Dean & Charles Diamond, 1001 Nights, JFL Theatricals/GHF Productions, Scott & Brian Zeilinger / James Lefkowitz.

INTERNATIONAL TOUR

Until 7 Jun
Not I / Footfalls / Rockaby
by Samuel Beckett

★★★★★
"Stunning. Moving. Chilling"
Daily Telegraph

Perth Festival, Hong Kong Arts Festival, Athenee Theatre Paris, Barbican Centre.

Presented by the Royal Court Theatre and Lisa Dwan in association with Cusack Projects Ltd.

BROADWAY

Until 15 Mar
Constellations
by Nick Payne

Nick Payne's critically acclaimed play with Jake Gyllenhaal and Ruth Wilson.

★★★★★
"Universal in every sense of the word" New York Times

Samuel J. Friedman Theatre, Manhattan.

Manhattan Theatre Club and the Royal Court Theatre in association with ATG and Dodger Properties.

020 7565 5000 (no booking fee)
royalcourttheatre.com

Follow us 🐦 royalcourt 📘 royalcourttheatre
Royal Court Theatre Sloane Square London, SW1W 8AS

INTERNATIONAL PLAYWRIGHTS
AT THE ROYAL COURT THEATRE

Over the last two decades the Royal Court has led the way in the development and production of new international plays, facilitating work at grass-roots level and developing exchanges which bring young writers and directors to work with emerging artists around the world. Through a programme of long-term workshops and residencies, in London and abroad, a creative dialogue now exists with theatre practitioners from over 70 countries, working in over 40 languages, most recently Chile, Cuba, Georgia, India, Iran, Lebanon, Mexico, Palestine, Russia, South Africa, Syria, Turkey, Ukraine and Zimbabwe. All of these development projects are supported by the Genesis Foundation and the British Council.

The Royal Court has produced dozens of new international plays through this programme since 1997, most recently **The Djinns of Eidgah** by Abhishek Majumdar (India) and **A Time to Reap** by Anna Wakulik (Poland) in 2013, **Remembrance Day** by Aleksey Scherbak (Latvia) and **Our Private Life** by Pedro Miguel Rozo (Colombia) in 2011, **Disconnect** by Anupama Chandrasekhar (India) in 2010.

THE ROYAL COURT IN PALESTINE

The Royal Court Theatre has worked in Palestine for more than 17 years, working with dozens of playwrights and running long-term projects in collaboration with local theatre artists including Al Kasaba Theatre in Ramallah and Al Harah Theatre in Beit Jala.

The first residential workshop took place at the Paradise Hotel in Bethlehem in February 1998, led by playwright Stephen Jeffreys, director Phyllida Lloyd and Royal Court International Director Elyse Dodgson. Since then numerous projects have been developed throughout the West Bank and many Royal Court writers and directors have taken part including April De Angelis, David Greig, Rufus Norris, and Sacha Wares. At the same time Palestinian artists have come to work with us as part of the Royal Court International Residency including Raeda Ghazaleh, Imad Farajin and most recently Dalia Taha who first began working on **Fireworks** in the summer of 2013.

In November 2013, 15 young playwrights from the West Bank and Gaza were invited to take part in a series of new workshops supported by the British Council and the A.M. Qattan Foundation in Beit Jala. These workshops were led by Mike Bartlett, Elyse Dodgson, Penelope Skinner and Richard Twyman. As a result, excerpts of eight new plays for Palestine were presented at Ashtar Theatre, Ramallah in November 2014.

The Genesis Foundation supports the Royal Court's International Playwrights Programme. It funds the International department's workshops in diverse countries as well as residencies at the Royal Court that find and develop the next generation of professional playwrights. The Foundation's involvement extends to productions and rehearsed readings which helps the Royal Court to provide a springboard for young writers to greater public and critical attention. For more information, please visit: www.genesisfoundation.org.uk

Genesis
FOUNDATION

THE ROYAL COURT THEATRE

The Royal Court Theatre is the writers' theatre. It is the leading force in world theatre for energetically cultivating writers – undiscovered, new, and established.

Through the writers the Royal Court is at the forefront of creating restless, alert, provocative theatre about now, inspiring audiences and influencing future writers. Through the writers the Royal Court strives to constantly reinvent the theatre ecology, creating theatre for everyone.

We invite and enable conversation and debate, allowing writers and their ideas to reach and resonate beyond the stage, and the public to share in the thinking.

Over 120,000 people visit the Royal Court in Sloane Square, London, each year and many thousands more see our work elsewhere through transfers to the West End and New York, national and international tours, residencies across London and site-specific work.

The Royal Court's extensive development activity encompasses a diverse range of writers and artists and includes an ongoing programme of writers' attachments, readings, workshops and playwriting groups. Twenty years of pioneering work around the world means the Royal Court has relationships with writers on every continent.

The Royal Court opens its doors to radical thinking and provocative discussion, and to the unheard voices and free thinkers that, through their writing, change our way of seeing.

Within the past sixty years, John Osborne, Arnold Wesker and Howard Brenton have all started their careers at the Court. Many others, including Caryl Churchill, Mark Ravenhill and Sarah Kane, have followed. More recently, the theatre has found and fostered new writers such as Polly Stenham, Mike Bartlett, Bola Agbaje, Nick Payne and Rachel De-lahay and produced many iconic plays from Laura Wade's **Posh** to Bruce Norris' **Clybourne Park** and Jez Butterworth's **Jerusalem**. Royal Court plays from every decade are now performed on stage and taught in classrooms across the globe.

It is because of this commitment to the writer that we believe there is no more important theatre in the world than the Royal Court.

Supported using public funding by
**ARTS COUNCIL
ENGLAND**

ROYAL COURT SUPPORTERS

The Royal Court is a registered charity and not-for-profit company. We need to raise £1.7 million every year in addition to our core grant from the Arts Council and our ticket income to achieve what we do.

We have significant and longstanding relationships with many generous organisations and individuals who provide vital support. Royal Court supporters enable us to remain the writers' theatre, find stories from everywhere and create theatre for everyone.

We can't do it without you.

Coutts supports Innovation at the Royal Court. The Genesis Foundation supports the Royal Court's work with International Playwrights. Alix Partners support The Big Idea at the Royal Court. Bloomberg supports Beyond the Court. The Jerwood Charitable Foundation supports emerging writers through the Jerwood New Playwrights series. The Pinter Commission is given annually by his widow, Lady Antonia Fraser, to support a new commission at the Royal Court.

PUBLIC FUNDING

Arts Council England, London
British Council

CHARITABLE DONATIONS

The Austin & Hope Pilkington
   Charitable Trust
Martin Bowley Charitable Trust
Cowley Charitable Trust
The Dorset Foundation
The Eranda Foundation
Lady Antonia Fraser for
   The Pinter Commission

Genesis Foundation
The Golden Bottle Trust
The Haberdashers' Company
The Idlewild Trust
Roderick & Elizabeth Jack
Jerwood Charitable
   Foundation
Marina Kleinwort Trust
The Andrew Lloyd Webber
   Foundation
John Lyon's Charity
Clare McIntyre's Bursary
The Andrew W. Mellon
   Foundation
The David & Elaine Potter
   Foundation
Rose Foundation
Royal Victoria Hall Foundation
The Sackler Trust
The Sobell Foundation
John Thaw Foundation
The Vandervell Foundation
Sir Siegmund Warburg's
   Voluntary Settlement
The Garfield Weston
   Foundation
The Wolfson Foundation

CORPORATE SPONSORS

AKA
AlixPartners
Aqua Financial Solutions Ltd
Bloomberg
Colbert
Coutts
Fever-Tree
Gedye & Sons
MAC

BUSINESS MEMBERS

Annoushka
Auerbach & Steele Opticians
Byfield Consultancy
CNC – Communications &
   Network Consulting
Cream
Heal's
Lazard
Salamanca Group
Vanity Fair

DEVELOPMENT ADVOCATES

Elizabeth Bandeen
Piers Butler
Sindy Caplan
Sarah Chappatte
Cas Donald (Vice Chair)
Celeste Fenichel
Piers Gibson
Emma Marsh (Chair)
Deborah Shaw
   (Vice Chair)
Tom Siebens
Sian Westerman

INDIVIDUAL SUPPORTERS

Major Donors
Eric Abraham
Ray Barrell & Ursula Van Almsick
Rob & Siri Cope
Cas Donald
Lydia & Manfred Gorvy
Richard & Marcia Grand
Jack & Linda Keenan
Adam Kenwright
Mandeep Manku
Miles Morland
Mr & Mrs Sandy Orr
NoraLee & Jon Sedmak
Deborah Shaw &
Stephen Marquardt
Jan & Michael Topham
Monica B Voldstad

Mover-Shakers
Anonymous
Christine Collins
Jordan Cook
Piers & Melanie Gibson
Duncan Matthews QC
Mr & Mrs Timothy D Proctor
Ian & Carol Sellars

Boundary-Breakers
Anonymous
Katie Bradford
David Harding
Madeleine Hodgkin
Mr & Mrs Roderick Jack
Nicola Kerr
Philip & Joan Kingsley
Emma Marsh
Rachel Mason
Andrew & Ariana Rodger
Clive & Sally Sherling

Ground-Breakers
Anonymous
Moira Andreae
Mr & Mrs Simon Andrews
Nick Archdale
Charlotte Asprey
Elizabeth & Adam Bandeen
Michael Bennett
Sam & Rosie Berwick
Dr Kate Best
Christopher Bevan
Sarah & David Blomfield
Deborah Brett

Peter & Romey Brown
Joanna Buckenham
Clive & Helena Butler
Piers Butler
Sindy & Jonathan Caplan
Gavin & Lesley Casey
Sarah & Philippe Chappatte
Tim & Caroline Clark
Carole & Neville Conrad
Andrea & Anthony Coombs
Clyde Cooper
Ian & Caroline Cormack
Mr & Mrs Cross
Andrew & Amanda Cryer
Alison Davies
Roger & Alison De Haan
Matthew Dean
Sarah Denning
Polly Devlin OBE
Rob & Cherry Dickins
Denise & Randolph Dumas
Robyn Durie
Glenn & Phyllida Earle
Graham & Susanna Edwards
Mark & Sarah Evans
Celeste & Peter Fenichel
Margy Fenwick
The Edwin Fox Foundation
Dominic & Claire Freemantle
Beverley Gee
Nick & Julie Gould
Lord & Lady Grabiner
Jill Hackel & Andrzej Zarzycki
Carol Hall
Maureen Harrison
Sam & Caroline Haubold
Mr & Mrs Gordon Holmes
Kate Hudspeth
Damien Hyland
Suzie & David Hyman
Amanda & Chris Jennings
Melanie J Johnson
Nicholas Jones
Susanne Kapoor
David P Kaskel
& Christopher A Teano
Vincent & Amanda Keaveny
Peter & Maria Kellner
Steve Kingshott
Mr & Mrs Pawel Kisielewski
David & Sarah Kowitz
Daisy & Richard Littler
Kathryn Ludlow
Suzanne Mackie
Dr Ekaterina Malievskaia
& George Goldsmith

Christopher Marek Rencki
Mr & Mrs Marsden
Mrs Janet Martin
Andrew McIver
David & Elizabeth Miles
Barbara Minto
Takehito Mitsui
Angelie Moledina
Riley Morris
M. Murphy Altschuler
Peter & Maggie Murray-Smith
Ann & Gavin Neath CBE
Clive & Annie Norton
Kate O'Neill
Jonathan Och & Rita Halbright
Georgia Oetker
Adam Oliver-Watkins
Sir William & Lady Vanessa Patey
Andrea & Hilary Ponti
Annie & Preben Prebensen
Paul & Gill Robinson
Daniel Romualdez
Corinne Rooney
Sir Paul & Lady Ruddock
William & Hilary Russell
Sally & Anthony Salz
Bhags Sharma
Tom Siebens & Mimi Parsons
Andy Simpkin
Anthony Simpson & Susan Boster
Andrea Sinclair & Serge Kremer
Paul & Rita Skinner
Brian Smith
Saadi & Zeina Soudavar
Sue St Johns
The Ulrich Family
Constanze Von Unruh
Jens Smith Wergeland
Matthew & Sian Westerman
Mrs Alexandra Whiley
Anne-Marie Williams
Sir Robert & Lady Wilson
Katherine & Michael Yates

With thanks to our Friends, Stage-Taker, Ice-Breaker and Future Court members whose support we greatly appreciate.

EMPLOYEES
THE ROYAL COURT & ENGLISH STAGE COMPANY

Royal Court Theatre
Sloane Square,
London SW1W 8AS
Tel: 020 7565 5050
info@royalcourttheatre.com
www.royalcourttheatre.com

Artistic Director
Vicky Featherstone
Executive Producer
Lucy Davies

Associate Directors
Hamish Pirie, John Tiffany*, Lucy Morrison*
Artistic Associates
Ola Animashawun*, Emily McLaughlin*
Associate Artist
Chloe Lamford*
Trainee Director
Debbie Hannan‡
Associate Artists
Carrie Cracknell, Simon Godwin, Katie Mitchell
International Director
Elyse Dodgson
International Associate
Richard Twyman
International Administrator
Callum Smith*
Education Associate
Lynne Gagliano*
Education Apprentice
Maia Clarke

Literary Manager
Christopher Campbell
Deputy Literary Manager
Louise Stephens
Literary Administrator
Hayley Dallimore
Trainee Administrator
(Literary)
Ashiokai Omaboe§

Head of Casting
Amy Ball
Casting Associate
Louis Hammond

Head of Production
Niall Black
Production Manager
Tariq Rifaat
Production Assistant
Zoe Hurwitz
Head of Lighting
Jack Williams
Deputy Head of Lighting
Marec Joyce
Lighting Technicians
Jess Faulks, Matthew Harding
JTD Programmer & Operator
Laura Whitley

Head of Stage
Steven Stickler
Stage Deputy
Dan Lockett
Stage Chargehand
Lee Crimmen
Chargehand & Building Maintenance Technician
Matt Livesey
Head of Sound
David McSeveney
Sound & Video Deputy
Emily Legg
Sound Operator
Madison English
Technical Trainee
Ashley Lednor§
Head of Costume
Lucy Walshaw
Wardrobe Deputy
Gina Lee

General Manager
Catherine Thornborrow
Administrator
(Maternity Leave)
Holly Gladwell
Administrator
(Maternity Cover)
Minna Sharpe
Projects Manager
Chris James
Assistant to the Executive
Phoebe Eclair-Powell
Trainee Administrator
(Producing)
Cherrelle Glave§
Associate Producer
Daniel Brodie*
Community Producer
(Pimlico)
Chris Sonnex*
Community Producer
(Tottenham)
Adjoa Wiredu*
Finance Director
Helen Perryer
Finance Manager
Martin Wheeler
Finance Officer
Rachel Harrison*
Finance & Administration
Assistant
Rosie Mortimer

Head of Marketing
& Sales
Becky Wootton
Press & Public Relations
The Cornershop PR
Marketing Manager
Dion Wilson
Communications Trainees
**Katie Davison§
Rida Hamidou§,**

Sales Manager
Liam Geoghegan
Deputy Sales Manager
Sarah Murray
Box Office Sales
Assistants
Ryan Govin, Joe Hodgson, Helen Preddy* (Maternity Leave), Margaret Perry* (Maternity Cover)

Head of Development
(Maternity Leave)
Rebecca Kendall
Head of Development
(Maternity Cover)
Lucy Buxton
Senior Individual Giving
Manager
Sue Livermore*
Trusts & Foundations
Manager
Clare O'Hara*
Development Managers
Luciana Lawlor, Anna Sampson
Development Officer
Nadia Vistisen

Theatre Manager
Rachel Dudley
Senior Duty House
Manager
Maureen Huish
Theatre Assistant
Chris Sonnex*
Venue Operations
Apprentice
Naomi Wright
Duty House Managers
Florence Bourne, Elinor Keber, Tanya Shields
Bar & Kitchen Manager
Ali Christian
Deputy Bar &
Kitchen Manager
Robert Smael
Assistant Bar &
Kitchen Manager
Jared Thomas
Head Chef
Tim Jenner
Sous Chef
Mandy Fitzhugh

Bookshop Manager
Simon David
Bookshop Assistant
Vanessa Hammick*

Stage Door/Reception
Paul Lovegrove, Tyrone Lucas, Jane Wainwright

Thanks to all of our Ushers
and Bar & Kitchen staff.

§ Posts supported by
The Sackler Trust
Trainee Scheme
‡The post of Trainee
Director is supported
by an anonymous donor.
* Part-time.

Support the world's leading new writing theatre

By making a donation to the Royal Court you can help us to respond to new and established playwrights, and supply them with the time, resources and environment to follow their imagination and exceed their potential.

Help us to make the Royal Court the renowned international success that it is.

MAKE A DONATION

To make a donation to the Royal Court, please:

Call Anna Sampson on 020 7565 5049
Email annasampson@royalcourttheatre.com
Visit royalcourttheatre.com/support-us/make-a-donation

Dalia Taha
Fireworks
Translated by Clem Naylor

Characters

Khalid, *a man in his early forties*
Nahla, *Khalid's wife, late thirties*
Lubna, *Khalid and Nahla's daughter, eleven to twelve years old*
Ahmad, *a man in his late thirties*
Samar, *Ahmad's wife, mid to late thirties*
Khalil, *Ahmad and Samar's son, twelve to thirteen years old*

The play takes place in a Palestinian town in the early part of the twenty-first century.

Scene One

Lubna I wrote a poem.

Khalid You wrote a poem?

Pause.

I was thinking you'd been quiet.

Lubna Not a poem. A song.

Khalid Sing it to me.

Lubna I haven't written it yet. It's still in my head.

Khalid What's it about.

Lubna It's about someone who gets shot and then –

Khalid Gets shot?

Lubna I mean gets martyred, and when he's martyred –

Khalid There's a difference –

Lubna I know.

Khalid A big, big difference.

Lubna I know.

Khalid Do you know what the difference is?

Lubna Yes.

Khalid What's the difference?

Lubna When you get shot, you die and get put under the earth and you get eaten by worms. But when you're martyred, it doesn't hurt and you don't die. All the angels come and fly you up to the sky, and then they give you wings like theirs. And God gives you a house in heaven and when you go into it you find all your family there because God's made a copy of them from some angels, so you don't feel lonely while you're waiting for them. And then when your family die they come and live with you in your house in heaven even if they haven't been martyred.

Khalid   And why does God give martyrs wings?

Lubna   So they can fly down from the sky to the earth and visit their family in their dreams, so they don't miss them.

Khalid   Now tell me about the poem.

Lubna   The song.

Khalid   The song.

Lubna   It's about someone who's martyred . . . And the streets are covered in photos of him . . . And his mum's walking down the street – Dad . . .?

Khalid   What?

Lubna   I haven't dreamt about Ali for ages.

Khalid   How long?

Lubna   Why has he stopped visiting me?

Khalid   You probably do dream about him but sometimes when we wake up we forget.

Lubna   I remember my dreams. You're in them and Mum is, and my friends are but he's not.

Khalid   I sometimes dream. Then in the morning I can't remember what I've dreamt about.

Lubna   Maybe he loves the Lubna in the sky more than me?

Khalid   He loves her because he loves you. She's just a copy of you. Don't forget that.

Lubna   Maybe he's angry with me because I broke the frame of his picture and now you can't go out and get a new one.

Khalid   I'm sure he knows you didn't break it on purpose. Don't worry about it.

Lubna   He knows?

Khalid   Yes, he knows. The angels tell him everything.

Lubna   So why don't I dream about him?

Khalid Let me tell you something. I know you dream about him.

Lubna Seriously?

Khalid We hear you talking in your sleep.

Lubna I talk in my sleep?

Khalid You wouldn't know. Course not. We only heard it this week since you've been sleeping in our room. We hear you talking in your dreams every night.

Lubna Seriously?

Khalid We hear you talking to him.

Lubna To Ali?

Khalid Sometimes Mum wakes up in the night and thinks you're calling for her.

Lubna What do I say?

Khalid Yesterday you were talking to him about Eid, how close it is. And how you're really happy because it's so soon.

Lubna But I'm not really happy.

Khalid Why not?

Lubna Because we're not going to the beach. And because there's no one for me to play with.

Khalid Why isn't there anyone for you to play with? Aren't you friends with the girl next door anymore?

Lubna They left.

Khalid When?

Lubna Today.

Khalid They'll come back before Eid. And anyway, we will go to the beach because everything will stop when it's Eid.

Lubna Has the Lubna in the sky got her Eid clothes?

Khalid   Have you?

Lubna   No.

Khalid   Then she hasn't got them yet either.

Lubna   They don't have bombs in the sky. They can go out.

Khalid   She only does what you do. They're sitting just like
we are right now.

Lubna   Is it daytime there?

Khalid   Yes.

Lubna   And they're talking about the same things?

Khalid   They're talking about us like we're talking
about them.

Lubna   But they don't have bombs.

Khalid   There aren't any bombs here either. They're
miles away.

Pause.

Lubna   What will happen to her when I die? Will she die?

Khalid   No.

Lubna   Why not?

Khalid   She'll go back to being an angel. Like she was
before . . . What are we doing here anyway? Let's go and
help Mum with the cake for Eid.

Lubna   Will Ali miss her?

Khalid   No, because he won't notice . . . (*Pause.*) And
anyway you won't die for a really, really, really long time.

Lubna   Really long?

Khalid   Yes.

Lubna   Not soon?

Khalid   No. What's got into your head?!

Lubna   Why did our neighbours leave?

Khalid   I told you – they'll be back soon . . . Don't you want to come with me? You like making cake.

Lubna   They were carrying bags with them.

Khalid   Were they?

Lubna   Yes.

Khalid   Of course – they were probably going to visit relatives for Eid.

Lubna   You said it was dangerous to leave the house.

Khalid   There are times when it's not dangerous to leave the house.

Lubna   My friend told me that her dad was taking them somewhere safe.

Khalid   Your friend's dad doesn't know –

Lubna   Is our building not safe?

Pause.

Khalid   Can you see that tape on the windows?

Lubna   Yes . . . It's a nice colour.

Khalid   That's magic tape. We got it specially from America. It protects our home and stops anything getting in. Nothing can break it.

Lubna   Did they leave their home because they don't have magic tape?

Khalid   Exactly . . . They went to another house where they have magic tape.

Lubna   So it's safe?

Khalid   Of course our home is safe . . . Would I keep you here if it wasn't?

Lubna   Can I sleep in my room tonight?

Khalid   Let me tell you something. Tonight we'll all sleep in your room. How about that? Come on, let's go and help Mum. It'll be Eid soon and we're happy!

She nods her head.

Scene Two

Samar   Oh merciful, forgiving Lord, we do not ask You to undo what has been done, we only ask You to show us kindness. Oh Lord the ever-listening, the merciful.

Ahmad   What?

Samar   Aren't you going to?

Ahmad   What?

Samar   Pray.

Ahmad   Since when –

Samar   I can't remember – I can't remember any more . . . is there one in the house?

Ahmad   A prayer?

Samar   A Quran.

Ahmad   No, there isn't . . . There used to be . . .

Samar   We don't have a single Quran in the house?

Ahmad   No.

Samar   In the whole house?

Ahmad   There's one in the car.

Samar   Go and get it.

Ahmad   It's tiny. You wouldn't be able to read it.

Samar   Tiny?

Ahmad   It's a key ring.

Samar   The only Quran we have is a key ring?

Ahmad   It was a present.

Samar   From who?

Ahmad   Just a token, really.

Samar   From who?

Ahmad   Someone at work. When he came back from the Hajj.

Samar   And you left it in the car?

Ahmad   Yes, I left it in the glove compartment.

I don't know why he got me one anyway. He knows I don't believe.

Samar   You don't believe?

Ahmad   Yes, I don't believe.

Samar   It's not good not to have a Quran in the house. Go and get it. It'll protect us.

Ahmad   Since when?

Samar   What?

Ahmad   Since when have you believed in these things?

Samar   I always have.

Ahmad   Always?

Samar   Yes, I've always believed.

Ahmad   You've never prayed.

Samar   I pray in my head.

Ahmad   You believe in God?

Samar   I believe in everything.

Ahmad   In hell? In heaven? In angels? In –

Samar   Yes, in everything. I believe in everything. Go and get the Quran.

Ahmad   You think a key ring Quran is going to stop the rockets falling on our house?

Samar   If anything happens to us it'll be your fault.

Ahmad   My fault?

Samar   It's all a punishment.

Ahmad   What do you mean?

Samar   You blaspheme, you don't believe, you don't fast during Ramadan and you don't give money to the poor.

Ahmad   Is Khalil a punishment?

Samar   What?

Ahmad   Did God give us a son like him to punish us?

Samar   What do you mean?

Ahmad   Because I don't believe.

Samar   You think he's a punishment?

Ahmad   Didn't you say –

Samar   My son's a blessing. Do you think he's a punishment?

Ahmad   I'm asking you.

Samar   Is that what you think of him?

Ahmad   Not *him* exactly.

Samar   Then what?

Ahmad   The way he is . . . What he's like . . .

Samar   What do you mean, 'the way he is'?

Ahmad   His mind . . . Not him . . .

Samar   There's nothing wrong with his mind.

. . .

Is there something wrong with his mind?

Ahmad   . . .

Samar   What's wrong with him?

Ahmad   Does he hit you?

Samar   What?

Ahmad   Does he hit you or not?

Samar   He's just a bit tense at the moment, because his routine's suddenly changed.

Ahmad   So he throws a glass at your face.

Samar   He's never thrown a glass before.

Ahmad   Really?

Samar   He's never thrown a glass at my face before.

Ahmad   There's something wrong with him.

Samar   He's so sensitive and kind, he should be a doctor.

Ahmad   He's violent.

Samar   He gets tense when his routine changes. Because of the power cuts, because he can't watch his cartoons.

Ahmad   Is he still watching cartoons?

Samar   He loves cartoons . . . Ninja Turtles is his favourite.

Ahmad   He's got a moustache – you've got to stop treating him like a little boy.

Samar   He's still a baby.

Ahmad   What if they come in? Round up the men? Do you think telling them he's a baby will make a difference?

From today, no more cartoons. He should be watching the news. From today, he's called Khalil, not sweetie.

Pause.

Samar   Aren't you going to get the Quran?

Ahmad   No, I'm going to talk to Khalil.

Scene Three

Lubna *is running up the steps, panting, and counting.*

Lubna   73, 74, 75, 76 –

Khalil   Hi.

Lubna   76, 77 –

Khalil   Hi.

Lubna   77, 77.

Khalil   Hello.

Lubna   What?

Khalil   Hello, hi.

Lubna   Hi?

Khalil   Do you drink Coca-Cola?

Lubna   I'm busy.

Khalil   Do you like it when it's warm?

Lubna   What?

Khalil   Coca-Cola.

Lubna   No.

Khalil   Do you like it when it's cold?

Lubna   I don't like Coke.

She carries on climbing.

78, 79 –

Khalil   Shall I get you one?

Lubna   80, 81 –

Khalil   A Coca-Cola?

Lubna   No.

Khalil   I'll get you one with a straw.

Lubna   I don't like Coke. 81, 82, 83, 84 –

Khalil   I like drinking Coca-Cola with a straw in the evening.

But in the morning I like drinking it from the can.

Lubna   Coca-Cola?

Khalil   And sometimes I drink it in a glass.

Lubna   It's called Coke, not Coca-Cola.

Khalil   Coke?

Lubna   Yes, Coke. No one calls it Coca-Cola. 78, 79 –

Khalil   Mum calls it Coca-Cola.

Lubna   Who's your mum?

Khalil   Mum.

Lubna   What's her name?

Khalil   I don't know her name.

Lubna   You don't know your mum's name?

Khalil   I call her Mum.

Lubna   You're strange!

Khalil   Mum says I'm special.

Lubna   79, 80, 81, 82, 83.

Khalil   You're good at counting.

Lubna   Thanks.

Khalil   What are you counting?

Lubna   I'm doing exercise.

Khalil   Really good at counting.

Lubna   Thanks.

Pause.

I can count backwards too.

Khalil   Backwards?

Lubna   Just as fast. Shall I show you?

Khalil   OK.

Lubna   87, 86, 85, 83.

Khalil   Wow.

Lubna   Once I won a prize.

Khalil   You won a prize?

Lubna   In the talent show, my talent was counting backwards.

Khalil   What was the prize?

Lubna   A photo frame. But it wasn't fair.

Khalil   Why?

Lubna   Because the whole class got prizes. Even the girl whose talent was hopping on one leg.

Khalil   Do you know how to hop?

Lubna   Everyone knows how to hop.

I can hop and count backwards at the same time.

She starts climbing the stairs again.

84, 85, 86, 87 –

Khalil   If they cut off your leg, you won't be able to hop anymore.

Lubna   I know.

Khalil   I saw a girl with her leg cut off.

Lubna   Where?

Khalil   On the TV. My dad told me that it hurts a lot if they cut off your leg.

Lubna   How does he know?

Khalil   I said 'Dad, does it hurt a lot if they cut off your leg?' And he said 'Yes, it really, really hurts.'

Do you want to be my friend?

Lubna   I have a friend.

Khalil   If you were my friend I'd let you feed my cat.

Lubna   Have you got a cat?

Khalil   Yeah . . . I found it yesterday . . .

Lubna   Is it little or big?

Khalil   Little.

Lubna   I love little cats. What colour is it?

Khalil   Mmmm . . . I don't know. Lots of colours.

Lubna   And does it meow?

Khalil   He doesn't speak . . . But he has really big eyes.

Lubna   Show me it.

He opens a box and shows her a dead pigeon.

Khalil   Do you like him?

Lubna   Yes.

Pause.

But it's not a cat.

Khalil   I call him cat.

Lubna   It doesn't look like a cat.

Khalil   He's called cat.

Lubna   Is it dead?

He starts putting some food into its mouth.

Khalil   He's ill because he's injured.

Lubna   Oh.

Khalil   I'm his doctor.

Lubna   I can be his doctor too.

Khalil   You're his mum.

Lubna OK.

Khalil   No, I'm his uncle and you're his doctor. His uncle didn't die because he was at his neighbour's house. We have to let him sleep now. You'll come and see him tomorrow.

She walks away. He puts the pigeon to sleep. He hits it.

Lubna   What are you doing?

Khalil   Nothing.

Lubna   You were hitting him?

Khalil   No.

Lubna   I saw you hitting him.

Khalil   You didn't see me because I didn't hit him.

Lubna   We have cameras and we can see everything.

Khalil   I only did it gently.

Lubna   No you did it hard.

Khalil   I didn't do it hard. He didn't bleed.

Lubna   It's not nice.

Khalil   I don't like hitting him but sometimes he doesn't do what I say. But when I hit him he always does what I say.

Lubna   What doesn't he do?

Khalil   He keeps on screaming and I can't sleep.

Lubna   He's screaming because his leg was cut off. We'll give him an injection so he can sleep.

Khalil   His leg was cut off?

Lubna Yes.

Khalil   But he likes to run.

Pause.

Will he be sad when he finds out his leg's been cut off?

Lubna   Maybe a bit sad.

Khalil   He's got flashing trainers and the lights go red when he runs. He runs to school. He really likes running.

Lubna   But there aren't any schools anymore.

Khalil   Really?

Lubna   The school's been bombed.

Khalil   They'll build a new one and he'll be the only boy in the school without a leg. And all the children will laugh at him and start calling him Mr One Leg, Mr One Leg.

Lubna   We'll take him to a special school, where all the children have their legs cut off, and no one will tease him because they'll all have one leg.

Khalil   He won't miss his mum?

Lubna   No ... Because his mum's in the sky and she'll visit him in his dreams every night.

Khalil   But she's not in the sky . . . She's under the rubble.

Lubna   Was he under the rubble too?

Khalil   Yes . . . I rescued him.

Lubna   Tell me how he was rescued.

Khalil   I don't want to.

Lubna   I want to know how it feels to be under the rubble.

Khalil   You're under the rubble and then someone comes and rescues you and you're not under the rubble anymore.

Lubna   But does it hurt?

Khalil   I don't know. Hey look – I have muscles. I rescue all the children because I've got big muscles.

Lubna   They're not big. I should go.

Khalil   Are you my friend now?

Lubna OK.

Khalil   If you're my friend we have to tell each other our secrets.

Lubna   Why?

Khalil   Because that's what friends do.

Lubna   I don't have any secrets.

Khalil   You must have a secret.

Lubna   No.

Khalil   Not one secret at all?

Lubna   I've got one.

Khalil   What?

Lubna   There's another Lubna who looks exactly like me.

Khalil   Wow.

Lubna   She lives in the sky ... And she's really happy.

Scene Four

Nahla   And this is him when he was seven.

Samar   Only seven?

Nahla   He looks older, doesn't he?

Samar   Yes.

Nahla   He always knew what he wanted.

Samar   Yes.

Nahla   He was different to all the other little boys.

Samar   Yes.

Nahla   He was never interested in football or
computer games.

Samar   Of course . . .

Nahla   I don't have many pictures. I didn't know.

Samar   Pictures aren't important.

Nahla   If I'd known how short his life would be, I would
have taken more.

Samar   Of course . . .

Nahla   Tell me again.

Samar   What?

Nahla   What happened in the dream?

Samar   I've told you twice.

Nahla   I want to hear it again.

Samar   I was driving the car and then I looked in
the mirror.

Nahla   Yes, you looked in the rear-view mirror.

Samar   And I saw someone sitting in the back.

Nahla   Someone laughing?

Samar   Sorry?

Nahla   You told me you saw someone laughing in the back.

Samar   Yes, yes, someone laughing.

And he said to me –

Nahla   But you didn't hear him laughing, you only realised
he was laughing when you saw him in the rear-view mirror.

Samar   Yes, I couldn't hear him.

Nahla   He kept on laughing.

Samar   And then I turned to look.

He said, 'Don't stop the car. You've got to carry on driving.'

Nahla   And then you saw the blood?

Samar   Yes, then I saw the blood. A pool of blood on
the seat.

Nahla   You didn't touch?

Samar   Your son?

Nahla   The blood.

Samar   No, I didn't touch it.

Nahla   Because that's bad.

Samar   What?

Nahla   Touching blood in a dream is bad.

Samar   No, I didn't touch it, but I was scared.

Nahla   You were scared and thought he was injured.
Injured and bleeding.

Samar   Yes, I thought he was injured.

Nahla   But he wasn't injured?

Samar   No.

Nahla   Are you sure?

Samar   Yes, I'm sure. He told me . . .

Pause.

Nahla   I think he's angry with me.

Samar   Angry?

Nahla   It's been a while since I visited him.

Samar   He didn't look angry.

Nahla   You don't know him. He laughs even when he's angry. You're not his mother.

Samar   He didn't seem angry.

Nahla   You have to tell him I can't leave the house . . . That's why I've been away.

Samar   I don't know if I'll have another dream about him –

Nahla   He clearly wants to tell you something. Take these pictures.

Take them and have a good look at them before you go to sleep.

Samar   OK.

Nahla   Try to understand what he wants . . . Tell him what's happening and tell him to come back and visit me.

Say 'Mum needs you.' . . . Tell him as soon as things get better I'll go and visit him . . . I'll come at Eid. Tell him I'll spend a whole day with him. Tell him 'Mum will spend a whole day with you.'

Samar   I'll see . . . I'll try –

Nahla   OK, go on.

Samar   What?

Nahla   Go and sleep.

Samar   It's so early.

Nahla   You have to sleep and dream. Go home. Have a cup of tea and go to sleep . . . Look at those bags under your eyes. I don't want you to meet my son with those bags under your eyes. You'll scare him . . . My son, my darling, my angel . . . My son, my darling, my angel.

Scene Five

Nahla   If only it wasn't a sin.

Khalid   It's not, in your case.

Nahla   I would've just thrown myself out of the window.

Khalid   You want to throw yourself out of the first floor?

Nahla   I would've killed myself the moment I heard the news.

Khalid   You wouldn't die from the first floor.

Nahla   I wouldn't have lived a minute longer than him.

Khalid   You'd just be paralysed.

Nahla   Shut up.

Khalid   You're not going to die from the first floor.

Nahla   Do you think I'm stupid?

Khalid   I'd have to carry you to the toilet every time you need a piss.

Nahla   I'm not going to throw myself out of the first floor.

Khalid   You're not going to die.

Nahla   I know I'm not going to die if I throw myself out of the first floor.

Khalid   You'd just break your legs.

Nahla   I'd go upstairs. Up onto the roof.

Khalid   You just said from the window.

Nahla   Don't worry – if I want to kill myself, I'll make sure.

Khalid   Make sure?

Nahla   Make sure I die. I'm not going to end up paralysed so you can rape me whenever you feel like it.

Khalid   I'm still your husband. You do remember that?

Nahla   You don't get it, do you?

Khalid   You've totally lost it.

Nahla   You're not his mother. You didn't carry him inside you for nine months. You can't understand how much it hurts for a mother.

Khalid   Seven.

Nahla   He wasn't born at seven months.

Khalid   He was born at seven months.

Nahla   You think you know my body better than me?

Khalid   I can remember.

Nahla   Nine . . . Exactly nine months.

Khalid   Because you didn't let me close to you for seven months.

Nahla   You're filthy.

Khalid   You're filthy.

Nahla   I'm talking about our son, our son who was martyred, and all you can think about is filth.

You couldn't even leave his room alone.

Khalid   Shut up.

Nahla   You think if you take a room and put some radios in it, you turn into an engineer.

Khalid   An electrician. I'm not an engineer.

Nahla   The neighbours give you things they don't want because they feel sorry for you.

Khalid   Stop.

Nahla   You've never fixed anything. Have they ever come back and asked you about their things?

Khalid   They know they need some work. They can't be sorted just like that.

Nahla   Do you think anyone really believes that you used to work as an engineer over there?

Khalid   Electrician.

Nahla   Let's make it like it was.

Khalid   What?

Nahla   His room . . . Let's put his things back in it.

Khalid   We don't have them anymore.

Nahla   We do. They're all in the store-room.

Khalid   Didn't you give them to charity?

Nahla   I lied . . . I didn't give anything away.

Pause.

Khalid   Don't you dare go near my room. You understand? Don't you dare.

Nahla   I'm going to make it like it was.

Khalid   Don't you dare go in. I need to give people their things back. I've nearly finished fixing them.

Nahla   The things they haven't asked you about for months.

Khalid   They're not in a rush.

Nahla   Tidy your things up or I'll throw them out the window.

Khalid   I'll kill you.

Nahla   Go ahead. Kill me. Leave me in peace.

Khalid   I won't kill you. I'll throw you out of the first floor.

Nahla   You're a failure.

Khalid   I'll turn you into a cripple. You'll have to beg me to take you to the toilet.

Nahla   A failure.

Khalid   And I won't take you. I won't take you to the toilet. I'll leave you to fill the whole house with piss. The whole house apart from my room.

Scene Six

Samar *jumps from the sofa onto the ground. She lies on the floor.* **Khalil** *laughs. She starts to get up and look around the flat as if she's exploring. She's dressed like a ninja turtle, her outfit made of plastic bags and clothes. She talks like she's a cartoon character.*

Samar   Where am I? What is this strange place? My God . . . My God, where am I?

He laughs.

This must surely be another planet . . . Oh, hello, I am a ninja turtle. Who are you?

Khalil   I'm – hahaha. I'm Khalil.

Samar   What are you doing here, Khalil?

Khalil   I'm the hero. I'm defending the homeland.

Samar   What is this place? It must be . . . What is this place?

Khalil   This is the tunnel. Can't you smell? That's what tunnels smell like.

Samar   No. It must be another planet.

Khalil   I built it myself. I dug every day and night until my hands were bleeding.

Samar   What's that? What's that strange machine? Is it for contacting the other world?

Khalil   How did you get into the tunnels?

Samar   Can you contact the other world? So they will come and help us.

Khalil   No . . . It's not allowed . . . If you call anyone they'll bomb us and we'll die.

Samar   Radio? Hello, hello, home world, we are stuck on a strange planet.

Khalil   No, don't call . . .

He takes the handset and throws it onto the floor.

Samar   Why did you do that?

Khalil   Shhh. If you call anyone they'll bomb us and we'll die in the tunnel.

Samar   But this is a planet. Yes, look at the map – I took off from Mars and now I think I must be on Saturn?

Khalil   Give it back. That's my map.

Samar   I'm sorry.

Khalil   It's the only map of the tunnels. Spy.

Samar   But this is another planet. It's not a tunnel.

Khalil   You're a spy. You have to die now. I'm going to kill you.

Samar   Please don't . . . I'm hungry.

Khalil   We've got food but I'm not going to give you any.

Samar   Why?

Khalil   I'm going to give it out to the people under siege. Because they're hungry.

Samar   I'm hungry too . . . I want to eat.

Khalil   Spy.

He shoots at his mother with his hand.

Bang bang bang bang.

She falls to the ground. He moves towards her. He takes her sword and laughs. Then he stops laughing, waiting for his mother to wake up.

Mum?

Mum?

Wake up, Mum . . . My head hurts . . .

Mum?

I want to go outside . . .

He moves away. She wakes up and runs at him, laughing.

I don't want to play.

Samar   I am the great ninja turtle. Are you going to leave me alone here?

Khalil   I don't want to play. You weren't really dead.

Samar   I pretended to be dead. I am invincible!

Khalil   I stole your sword.

Samar   A-ha, so you took my sword.

Khalil   When you were sleeping. You shouldn't have let me steal it.

Samar   Well . . . I'll give you the sword. You deserve it because you are a hero and you help the people of your town.

Khalil   You shouldn't have let me take your sword.

Samar   I will take it back.

Khalil   You should have bitten me.

Samar   Bitten you?

Khalil   Now I can kill you and leave the house and go to the internet café.

Samar   We cannot leave this planet.

Khalil   If you'd bitten me I wouldn't have taken the sword. Why didn't you bite me?

Samar   Because I was dead.

Khalil   You weren't really dead.

Samar (*back to being herself*)   None of this is real. It's all pretending.

Khalil   But when I play computer games, I really die.

Samar   Do you want me to really die?

Pause.

Khalil   I don't know.

Samar   If I really died you and Dad would have to live on your own.

Khalil   But you'd still talk to me.

Samar   I wouldn't be able to talk to you.

Khalil   If I died, I'd carry on talking to you . . . Because I love you.

Samar   You wouldn't be able to talk to me.

Khalil   Why?

Samar   Because you'd be buried in the ground.

Khalil   I'd go into the tunnels.

Samar   And sleep alone? You want to stop sleeping with me?

Khalil   We could die together?

Samar   That's why we have to stay together.

Khalil   Come on, then, come with me to the internet café.

Samar   But we don't want to die . . . Do you want to die?

Khalil   I want to be martyred.

Samar   Why?

Khalil   I don't know. Stop asking me questions . . . I wouldn't mind if you were martyred . . .

Samar   Why not?

Khalil   Because I'd see you on TV.

Samar   But maybe I'd be like that boy whose dad picked him up and put him in a plastic bag.

Khalil   . . .

Samar   Do you want to pick up my arms and legs and put them in a plastic bag?

Khalil   No I don't. Dad will pick you up, not me . . . Tell him that he has to pick you up.

Samar   And do you want me to pick you up and put you in a plastic bag?

Khalil   No.

Samar   That's why you're not going to play with your friends until the war stops. And the war's nearly over . . . When it's Eid, you can go on the internet and play as much as you like.

Khalil   OK.

Samar   Do you promise?

Khalil   You'll tell Dad that he has to pick you up, not me?

Samar   Of course I'll tell him . . . Do you think I'm that horrible? To leave you to pick me up bit by bit . . . I'll tell Dad he'll have to do it . . . Come on, then, let's play some more ninja turtles . . . We're on a planet, far, far away. Just me and you. No one else there. What should we call it?

Scene Seven

4 a.m., **Lubna, Khalid** *and* **Nahla** *are sleeping in the same room.* **Lubna** *gets up and goes towards the door.* **Khalid** *wakes up.*

Khalid   Are you going to the bathroom?

Lubna   No.

Khalid   For a drink?

Lubna   No. I had some water.

Khalid   Where are you going?

Lubna   To watch the fireworks.

Khalid   Without telling me?

Lubna   I thought you were asleep.

Khalid   I was, but you woke me up.

Lubna   Sorry.

Khalid   I like watching the fireworks too.

Lubna   I know.

Khalid   Why would you go without me? Do you want to make me sad?

Lubna   I couldn't sleep.

Khalid   Haven't you got your earplugs in?

Lubna   No.

Khalid   Why not? Put them in; you'll be able to sleep.

Lubna   I gave them to Mum.

Khalid   Why?

Lubna   Because she hasn't slept for so long.

Khalid   You're a clever girl. But don't worry about Mum – she'll sleep.

Lubna   She's got such big bags under her eyes.

Khalid   She's just a bit tired because she's got so much to do before Eid . . . I'll get her another pair of earplugs.

Lubna   I thought if she slept a bit she'd get better.

Khalid   What do you mean get better?

Lubna   She's going crazy.

Khalid   Crazy? What made you think that?

Lubna   She imagines things that aren't there.

Khalid   Your mum?

Lubna   Sometimes she shouts for Ali.

Pause.

Khalid   Oh! That's because she's still used to calling his name . . . She still hasn't –

Lubna   But he's been dead for six months.

Khalid   For you six months is a long time, because you're little, but for grown ups it's not long at all.

Lubna   You don't shout his name by mistake.

Khalid   Mothers are more used to calling their children's names than fathers.

Lubna   She's not imagining things and seeing things that aren't there?

Khalid   No! She's not imagining things and seeing things that aren't there. She's just not used to not having your brother around. Don't you call for Dad even when I'm not there?

Lubna   She always keeps the curtains closed too.

Khalid   I know it's summer . . . But keeping the curtains closed doesn't mean you're going crazy.

Lubna   She says she doesn't like the sky when it's red. Only when it's not red.

Khalid   She just doesn't like fireworks. She's not like us . . . Do you remember when there were fireworks for Ramadan and you and me went up on the roof to watch and she stayed downstairs being grumpy.

Lubna   Grandma used to say she didn't like the sky when it was red.

Khalid   Grandma didn't go crazy . . . She just got really old. Of course you couldn't sleep, worrying that Mum was going crazy.

Lubna   Grandma used to go out and not know how to get home.

Khalid   That's because she was so old . . . Come and sleep next to me.

Lubna   Mum looks like she wants to go away. (*Pause.*)

I saw her putting money and jewellery and passports into a bag. And when I asked her why she was packing, she told me it was because we were going away.

Khalid   Did she?

Lubna   No one can go away now. All the roads are blocked . . . aren't they?

Khalid   I wanted it to be a surprise but it looks like you already found out.

Lubna   What sort of surprise?

Khalid   I told Mum to pack the bag. We might go away at Eid.

Lubna   Really?

Khalid   Yes, yes, yes! Anywhere you like . . . You get to decide.

Lubna   Let Mum decide.

Khalid   In the morning we'll speak to Mum and ask her where she wants to go.

Lubna   And tell her the sky's not red too.

Khalid   I'll tell her.

Lubna   And that the war's far away . . . Cos she's always scared and once I heard her saying 'Please God don't take Lubna away like you took Ali.'

Khalid   You heard her say that?

Lubna   Tell her I won't die for ages.

Khalid   I'll tell her in the morning. I'll tell her as soon as she wakes up.

Lubna   You keep telling me these things and I already know them, but she doesn't.

Khalid   OK.

Lubna   And tell her that the helicopters aren't scary. Yesterday I saw one with people in and I waved at the captain and they waved back.

Khalid   Really?

Lubna   Yes, I swear. Tell her they even said 'How are you?' and I said 'Fine' but they couldn't hear because they were flying.

Khalid   You're a clever girl, you know that?

Lubna   Yes.

Khalid   I don't want you worrying about these things. Mum's still really sad about your brother so sometimes she says strange things and does strange things.

Lubna   Is that why we're going away?

Khalid   Yes, yes, that's why.

Lubna   So we can make her happy again

Khalid   Exactly. As soon as it's Eid we'll go away and everything'll go back to normal.

Lubna   And the bags under her eyes will go away.

Khalid   If we don't sleep, we'll get bags under our eyes too. And you're still little and you don't want to have bags under your eyes, do you? If you get them when you're little then they never go away.

Lubna   Yeah, I don't want them because when I go to heaven I want to be pretty.

Scene Eight

Khalil *and* **Ahmad** *are on the roof feeding pigeons.*

Ahmad   It's nice up here.

Khalil   That building's gone.

Ahmad   Which building?

Khalil   The one that was there, with the green windows.

Ahmad   Yes.

Khalil   It was so big.

Ahmad   Yes.

Khalil   And that building that was there.

Ahmad   Yes.

Khalil   When I grow up I'm going to buy a big plane.

Ahmad   Haha. Why?

Khalil   So when they come and bomb us I can shoot down all their planes.

Ahmad   You want to be a pilot?

Khalil   And I want to fix cars.

Ahmad   Oh! Two jobs! You won't have time to come and visit your mum and dad.

Khalil   I'll be fixing cars then if someone calls to say we're being bombed I'll get in my plane and shoot whatever's bombing us.

Ahmad   Wow.

Khalil   Yes, like Superman and the Ninja Turtles. Then they'll be scared because they'll know I've got a big plane that can beat all their planes and there won't be a war ever again.

Ahmad   Can I be your co-pilot?

Khalil   No.

Ahmad   Why not?

Khalil   Lubna will come with me in the plane.

Ahmad   Who's Lubna?

Khalil   The girl from upstairs.

Ahmad   Oh, her.

Khalil   Will you and Mum buy the plane for me?

Ahmad   When you grow up you'll have money and you'll buy it for yourself.

Khalil   How will I get money?

Ahmad   You'll get a job.

Khalil   But you're a grown-up and you don't have a job.

Ahmad   I'll get a job again soon.

Khalil   Will you get a job when the war's over?

Ahmad   Yes.

Khalil   Because there are houses that have been bombed and you're going to re-build them?

Ahmad   Yes. And things will get better and better until you're grown-up. The siege will end. Then maybe you won't have to buy a plane.

Khalil   No, I want to buy a plane.

Ahmad   Where will you land it? We don't have an airport.

Khalil   On the roof.

Ahmad *laughs.*

Ahmad   What'll we do with our pigeons?

You like the pigeons, don't you?

Khalil   Yes I like them a lot. I always kiss them.

Ahmad   So why do you look sad?

Khalil   You told Mum you'd let them go.

Ahmad   Where would they go? We look after them, we feed them. What would happen to them if I let them go?

Khalil   Mum says people die because of pigeons.

Ahmad   . . .

Khalil   Is it true?

Ahmad   No.

Khalil   She said a family died because of their pigeons.

Ahmad   They didn't die because of the pigeons. (*Pause.*)
And no one's going to change the way we live our lives.
That's why we have to come and feed the pigeons. Even if it
means we have to lie to Mum.

Khalil   What if she smells me?

Ahmad   What?

Khalil   She'll smell me when I'm sleeping and she'll know
I've been with the pigeons and you haven't let them go.

Ahmad   I'll wash you when we go down.

OK?

Khalil   Fine.

Ahmad   What, don't you want me to wash you?

Khalil   It's not that.

Ahmad   You let Mum wash you.

Khalil   It's not that.

Ahmad   You shouldn't let her anymore. I'm going to
wash you.

Khalil   There isn't any water.

Ahmad   Oh . . . Yes.

Khalil   Did you forget?

Ahmad   Yes, I did. But you know what we're going to do
when we go downstairs? We're going to learn how to shave.
Because you're a man now. And men shave.

He points towards the pigeon **Khalil** *is holding.*

Is he your favourite?

Khalil   Yes.

Ahmad   Did you know pigeons can hear the wind thousands of miles away?

Khalil   No.

Ahmad   They can. So when you're holding a pigeon you're connected to the whole world, in a strange sort of way.

Khalil   Can he hear other things too?

Ahmad   Like what?

Khalil   Like someone screaming because they're hurt.

Ahmad   I think so.

Khalil   That's awful. Does that mean he can hear everyone who's screaming because they're hurt now?

Ahmad   He can hear other things too. Do you know what he's hearing right now? He's hearing the men shaving. All of them, preparing. He's hearing the sounds of little hairs falling gently on basins and covering them like black snow. If someone turned off every TV in every house – every TV that works – and if the shooting stopped for a moment, and if you listened, if you really listened carefully, you'd hear the sound of electric razors buzzing out from every house. You'd hear the sounds of children turning into men.

Suddenly, the humming of a warplane breaks through **Ahmad**'s *monologue. As it becomes louder and drowns out his voice, he quickly grabs* **Khalil**'s *hand and they rush off the roof.*

Ahmad   (*as if he remembers something suddenly on his way out*) There's one pigeon missing, the black one. Have you seen it?

Khalil   He flew away.

Scene Nine

Khalid   Aren't you going to open the door?

Nahla   No.

Khalid   Open it.

Nahla   I should be drinking my coffee now, not standing at the door.

Khalid   I want to get some batteries.

Nahla   And get shot?

Khalid   I'm not going to get shot. You know I'm not going to get shot.

Nahla   I'm not going to let you out.

Khalid   Your mum said that I'd die from a heart attack.

Nahla   I should be drinking my coffee and not thinking about anything . . . Lying in bed, not thinking about a thing. Not thinking about the fact that I have a husband like you.

Khalid   I want to see if my radios work.

Nahla   No way.

Khalid   No way?

Nahla   There's no way I'm going to let you get shot and see him before me.

Khalid   Give me the keys.

Nahla   No one in this family gets to die before me. No one.

Khalid   Open the door. You're mad.

Nahla   No one's asking for the fucking radios.

Khalid   I'd strangle you if I could, but I know nothing would make you happier.

Nahla   Strangle me.

Khalid   I want to go out.

Nahla   Take off your clothes.

Khalid   What?

Nahla   Take your clothes off quickly.

Khalid   Why?

Nahla   Do you want me to take them off for you?

Khalid   What?

Nahla   You can fuck me. But you cannot die before me.

Khalid   Here?

Nahla   Yes, here.

Scene Ten

Khalil *and* **Lubna** *are on the steps. He is carrying a stick and using it like it's a gun. She is standing still.*

Khalil   Git bach, git bach. Yalla, Yalla.

She moves backwards.

A long pause, with him walking about pretending to talk to his colleagues. He carries the stick, lifting it up as if he is aiming in a particular direction. He goes back to Lubna and shouts.

Git bach. Can't you hear me?

She says nothing and stands still.

ID.

She gives him a piece of paper. He throws it onto the ground. He whistles a tune. He is listening to music on a mobile phone and dancing to it. He walks about pretending to smoke a cigarette.

Nice music, isn't it?

Lubna   Yes.

Khalil   You like it, don't you?

Lubna   Yes.

He holds the mobile up to her ear.

Khalil Dance.

She doesn't answer.

If you don't dance I'll turn off the music.

She doesn't answer.

And if I turn off the music I'll get very angry and start shooting.

She starts dancing.

He starts laughing and clapping.

Laugh with me, you idiot.

She starts laughing.

He suddenly stops laughing.

Why are you laughing?

Lubna Because –

Khalil Have you got anything to laugh about? I've been standing here in the sun for three hours.

Lubna You –

Khalil You're only allowed to say 'yes' or 'no'.

Lubna No.

Khalil Liar.

Lubna Yes.

Khalil Liar. You were laughing just now.

Lubna I was about to sneeze.

Khalil You're lying to me, you idiot.

Lubna I looked like I was going to laugh but I was sneezing.

Khalil Why? Are you mad?

Lubna   I had an operation on my mouth once and whenever I'm about to sneeze it looks like I'm about to laugh.

Khalil   Show me . . . Sneeze.

She doesn't answer.

I said sneeze.

She sneezes.

Sneeze.

She sneezes.

Sneeze.

She sneezes.

I don't like the way you sneezed. So now you're going to stand on one leg.

He gets a cigarette out.

Do you want a cigarette?

Lubna   No thanks. I don't smoke.

Khalil   I'll only give you a cigarette if you do what I say.

Lubna   I don't want a cigarette.

Khalil   Ask me what the rule is?

Lubna   What?

Khalil   What's the rule?

Lubna   What's the rule?

Khalil   Repeat after me – what's the rule?

Lubna   What's the rule?

Khalil   Smoke it and when the smoke comes out suck it back in again.

She takes the cigarette, and starts smoking and trying to catch the smoke.

Now swallow mine and yours together.

She sucks in the smoke that's coming out of their cigarettes.

He starts smoking quickly to make it more difficult for her. She gets annoyed and suddenly pushes him. She takes the gun.

You can't do that.

Lubna   Yes I can.

Khalil   Now you're going to kill me and it'll all be over.

Lubna   I don't want to play this game. I don't like it.

Khalil   But I haven't searched you yet! Let's carry on till we get to the search. It's my favourite bit.

Lubna   I don't want to play.

Khalil   Why not?

Lubna   Because I don't get to say anything.

Khalil   But you don't need to say anything.

Lubna   I don't want not to say anything . . . It's boring.

Khalil   If you say anything I'll shoot you.

Lubna   It's boring . . . Why don't I get a gun too?

Khalil   Only the soldier gets a gun.

Lubna   OK, so I'll be the soldier and you can be the man.

Khalil   I know how to be the soldier and you don't.

Lubna   Then I don't want to play. I want to have a gun too. I just say yes and no and answer your questions.

Pause.

Khalil   OK. You can have a knife.

Lubna   A knife?

Khalil   But not a proper knife . . . Just a kitchen knife.

Lubna   And do you know that I've got it?

Khalil   Come on let's play again.

They get up again.

Git bach, git bach.

She moves back.

Git bach.

She moves towards him. He screams.

Git bach, git bach.

She continues to get closer to him. He starts shooting.

Khalil   BANG BANG BANG.

She falls to the ground.

He moves towards her.

There's blood on your trousers.

Scene Eleven

Nahla   Who told you to use TCP?

Lubna   I thought it was a cut.

Nahla   Half the bottle's gone.

Lubna   I thought I had a cut. My trousers were covered in blood.

Nahla   You can't put TCP on it.

Lubna   When I'm cut I always use TCP.

Nahla   Why has it happened so early?

Lubna   Isn't that right?

Don't I put TCP on cuts?

Nahla There's . . . I mean, down there, there's . . . Don't put . . . We really are so different.

Lubna Am I going to die?

Nahla Why would you die?

Lubna Because there's blood coming out of me.

Nahla Don't they teach you anything at school?

Lubna I don't know . . .

Nahla If you concentrated a bit more on your school work . . .

Lubna Mum.

Nahla You'd know why this was happening. Not one of your friends?

Lubna What?

Nahla No one's told you anything?

Lubna I don't have any friends. Isn't the blood going to stop?

Nahla What?

Lubna This is the third pair of trousers.

Nahla I thought you'd be like me . . . You'd be thirteen, fourteen.

Lubna What's wrong with me?

Nahla Haven't you learnt anything in Biology?

Lubna Am I ill?

Nahla Don't be silly.

Lubna I'm covered in blood. And the trousers you got from America are covered in blood too.

Nahla We can wash them.

Lubna   They shrink when you wash them; the last time you washed them they didn't fit.

Nahla   You've had them for two years. We should throw them out anyway.

Lubna   I'm going to die.

Nahla   You're not going to die.

Lubna   And you're not going to be able to take me to hospital.

Nahla   You're not going to die.

You're going to have to live with this shit all your life.

Once a month for the rest of your life.

It happens to me. And to everyone else.

Lubna   Blood comes out of you?

Nahla   Yes, and every other woman.

Lubna   Sana?

Nahla   Yes.

Lubna   And Susan?

Nahla   Yes.

Lubna   And Um Hassan?

Nahla   Yes. No. No, not Um Hassan.

Lubna   Why?

Nahla   Because . . . they took out her womb.

Lubna   What do you mean?

Nahla   She had cancer. They took it out.

Lubna   Was she ill?

Nahla   Yes.

Lubna   I've never seen them with dirty trousers.

Nahla   Because they use towels.

Lubna   Every month?

Nahla   Yes.

Lubna   All my life?

Nahla   Yes. I mean, until about –

Lubna   When?

Nahla   Yes, all your life.

Lubna   Once a month for the rest of my life, blood will come out of me?

Nahla   Yes.

Lubna   And my trousers will be ruined.

Nahla   No. You put . . . a towel. I don't have a small one. Put this in for now.

Lubna   What's that?

Nahla   Put it in and when it's full, you wrap it up like this in tissue.

Lubna   Why?

Nahla   To stop germs spreading.

Lubna   Wrap it?

Nahla   Don't put it in the bin without wrapping it up. And just be careful there's no sign of blood in the bin.

Lubna   Cover it all?

Nahla   Be careful so Dad can't see anything.

Lubna   What if you're lying to me?

Nahla   Lying to you?

Lubna   I don't believe blood can come out of me without me being ill.

Nahla   Ask your friends.

Lubna   Why didn't you tell me before?

Nahla   Why would I tell you before?

Lubna   So I could prepare myself. So I could know.

Nahla   It doesn't matter now.

Lubna   I could have been shamed in front of the whole school.

Pause.

What if I'd been at school? What if it had happened at school?

Today's Tuesday. I'm supposed to be at school now, in English.

And the teacher always gets me to come to the board . . . She gets me to answer because I always get it wrong.

And she likes to show the rest of the class the wrong answer first.

Imagine if I was standing at the board, in front of the whole class, covered in blood . . .

Nahla   Your answers are always wrong?

Lubna   You should have told me before.

Nahla   If you carry on like that, you'll be out of school in a couple of years.

Lubna   That'd be a good thing . . .

I hate you.

Nahla   Give me your trousers so I can wash them.

Lubna   I don't want them. Throw them away.

Nahla   You don't want your trousers from America?

Lubna   I don't want them. Burn them.

Scene Twelve

Lubna   I wish I could get cancer.

Khalil   What?

Lubna   Cancer. They take out your womb.

Khalil   Womb?

Lubna   Yes, womb.

Khalil   Have you got one?

Lubna   I think I got it recently.

Khalil   My mum's got one.

I'm going to tell her.

Lubna   Who?

Khalil   Mum. Tell her that you're like her.

Lubna   Everyone has a womb.

Khalil   What do you mean?

Lubna   When they're twelve they get a womb.

Khalil   What about me?

Lubna   Not you. Just women.

Khalil   All women?

Lubna   Except Um Hassan.

Khalil   Why?

Lubna   She got cancer. They took it out.

Khalil   They took it from her belly?

Lubna   Yes.

Khalil   And what's there now?

Lubna   I don't know. A gap . . . I don't think there's anything. I don't know what's there. I didn't ask my mum.

Khalil   And you want to have a gap inside you?

Lubna   That's not what I meant.

Khalil   But you're little. If you had yours out there would be a small gap.

Lubna   I think so . . .

Khalil   But it would grow when you grow.

Lubna   It would grow?

Khalil   The gap. It would grow. Don't you want to play?

Lubna   No.

What's the first thing you'll do when everything ends?

Khalil   The first thing I'll do?

Lubna   Yes. What's the thing you want to do most now?

Khalil   What do you mean?

Lubna   Like for me, the thing I want to do first is go to the ice cream shop and eat ice cream.

Khalil   I want to go and drink Coke.

Lubna   Not something like that.

Khalil   Why?

Lubna   It has to be something you can't do now.

Khalil   But I don't like ice cream.

Lubna   You don't have to go and eat ice cream, something else, something you like.

Khalil   I don't know.

Lubna   You don't know what you like?

Khalil   It's a difficult question.

Lubna   Aren't you looking forward to anything?

Khalil   What are you looking forward to?

Lubna   I'm looking forward to going to the ice cream shop. I'm looking forward to seeing my friend. But I'm not looking forward to my dabkeh classes.

Khalil   What's dabkeh?

Lubna   You don't know dabkeh?

Khalil   Is it a kind of food?

Lubna   No, it's a kind of dance. Other people like it, but I don't.

Khalil   You dance?

Lubna   My mum only lets me go to it so I'll lose weight.

Khalil   Oh?

Lubna   Because the gym's expensive. Dabkeh's much cheaper.

But I don't like it. There's only one move – lift your foot up and put it down, lift it up and put it down.

Khalil   My mum lifts her foot up and puts it down when she's angry.

Lubna   You have to hold hands with the person next to you. And their hands are always sweaty. I hate holding sweaty hands.

Khalil   Why?

Lubna   It's disgusting. Boys' hands . . . And none of them wash after they go to the toilet. Do you wash your hands?

Khalil   I shower.

Lubna   Not when you shower. When you go to the toilet do you wash your hands?

Khalil   I can't remember.

Lubna   You can't remember.

Khalil   Smell.

Lubna   No.

Khalil   Smell my hair.

Lubna   I don't want to smell it.

Khalil   It smells of vanilla.

Lubna   I don't want to smell it . . . Come on, let's play.

Khalil   Let's dance dabkeh.

Lubna   No. Let's play a new game.

Khalil   The checkpoint game?

Lubna   No, the running game.

Khalil   What's the running game?

Lubna   We run outside.

Khalil   We can't run outside. It's not allowed.

Lubna   No one will see us. The streets are empty. I'll run this way and you run that way, and whoever gets to the front door first and doesn't get shot wins.

Scene Thirteen

Nahla   I got some cigarettes.

Khalid   What?

Nahla   Do you want one?

Khalid   You got cigarettes?

Nahla   I wanted to get candles . . . We're about to run out.
But there weren't any in the shop. Obviously everyone's
buying as many candles as they can. So I got cigarettes
instead.

Khalid   You went out?

Nahla   Yes.

Khalid   Yes?

Nahla   They're shitty smuggled ones.

Khalid   Shitty?

Nahla   Yes, shitty.

Khalid   Why are you telling me this?

Nahla   I'm trying to have a conversation with you.

Khalid   How did you get out?

Nahla   I opened the door.

Khalid   You just decided to open the door?

Nahla   It wasn't locked.

Khalid   I've never locked it

Nahla   No.

Khalid   Have I ever locked the door?

Nahla   No.

Khalid   I could have locked it, but I never have.

Nahla   I know, you are very sweet.

Khalid   Where did you get them from?

Nahla   Get what?

Khalid   The cigarettes?

Nahla   I told you, I bought them.

Khalid   You bought them?

Nahla   The man from the building opposite. He sells smuggled cigarettes.

Khalid   You walked in the street?

Nahla   It was hardly a walk.

Khalid   Yeah?

Nahla   Yeah I just crossed the street.

Khalid   And what did he say?

Nahla   Who?

Khalid   Abu Ahmad.

Nahla   Nothing. He just said, 'That'll be 100 shekels' or something.

Khalid   He didn't say anything like, 'How come your husband let you leave the house?'

Nahla   No.

Khalid   And you didn't say something like, something like, 'My husband is a son of a bitch and he'd barely notice if I got shot right in front of him.'

Nahla   I just said, 'Can I have three packets of cigarettes, please?' They were so expensive. Shame on him, taking advantage of people at a time like this.

Khalid   I know what people say behind my back.

Nahla   No one says anything about you.

Khalid   Yeah?

Nahla   It was a short, normal conversation between a customer and a salesman. He was in his pyjamas and his slippers and it happened in his living room, but other than that it was just a like any conversation you'd have with a shopkeeper.

Khalid   Then why were you gone for three hours?

Nahla   I went for a walk.

Khalid   You went for a walk?

Nahla   Yes, I went for a walk. I was crossing the street and I saw it was empty, and the cars were smashed. It's the first time I've seen the street empty like that. So I decided to walk.

Khalid   What were you thinking going out walking in the street?

Nahla   I needed to think.

Khalid   Think about what?

Nahla   Important things.

Khalid   Like what?

Nahla   Things.

Khalid   Like what? God? Life? War? Death? The price of tomatoes? How the trees look at night? The percentage of fat in your favourite yoghurt? Suffering? The state of the world? Children in Africa? What were you thinking about?

Nahla   I had to think about what the Kalashnikov was doing in my bedroom!

Khalid   It's a pistol.

Nahla   Why would someone like you hide a Kalashnikov in my bedroom? In the room where we used to have sex, and touch each other, and stare into each other's eyes. Where our children used to sleep between us. Where would someone like you get a Kalashnikov from?

Khalid   It's a pistol, not a Kalashnikov. A pistol. Kalashnikovs are for people who want to kill. This is just a pistol. Just to scare people.

Nahla   Yeah?

Khalid   Yeah yeah yeah yeah yeah yeah.

Nahla   Why do we have a pistol in the house?

Khalid   Just so we can feel safe.

Nahla   Safe?

Khalid   I don't even know how to use it.

Nahla   If you want to feel safe why don't we leave?

Khalid   And go where exactly?

Nahla   To one of the shelters. One of the schools where everyone's hiding . . . It's safe there. Everyone's leaving our building.

Khalid   It's not safe! . . . Only yesterday one of them was bombed.

Pause.

The graveyard was bombed.

Nahla   His graveyard?

Khalid   Yes.

Nahla   His graveyard?

Khalid   They bombed the graveyard.

Pause.

Nahla   Let's go.

Khalid   We can't.

Pause.

You know we can't.

Nahla   I'm going to see my son. My son who was martyred.

Khalid   He's not a martyr.

Long Pause.

Nahla   Don't ever say that my son is not a martyr.

Khalid   Baby, baby . . . don't go, don't go, please don't leave
. . . baby, everything's mad. Where are we? We could die any
second . . . People you trust. They're mad. We can't trust
anyone. We've got to be ready. Every morning I wake up
and I cough up blood. I spit blood. My insides are rebelling.
There's a revolution inside me. There are devils inside me
spitting blood. Can you – everything's going wrong. Baby,
he's not a martyr, he's just a boy who got killed. He got shot.
For no reason . . . No, no, no, don't go. Let's make his room
the way it was; let's put his things back. I don't want my
radios. I don't want them; throw them away. (*Pause.*) He
never even threw a stone . . . Some crazy soldier decided to
kill him just because he could . . . He's dead. He died. He
was killed. He's gone now . . . Martyred, killed, it doesn't
matter . . . Grave, no grave, it doesn't matter . . . He's gone.
Baby, we can't hide. You can't see what's happening . . . You
can't see the sky. You see the sky. I don't recognise the sky
anymore. It's red, it's red. I can't see the sky, WHERE IS
THE SKY? Everything's going to hell. Everything's going to
hell and the world will never be the same again . . . We'll
never be the same again.

Scene Fourteen

Ahmad *is washing* **Samar**. *She is in the bathtub. He is using
bottled water.*

Ahmad   Too cold?

Samar   It's fine. It makes me feel alive.

Ahmad   We haven't done this in a long time.

Samar   Do you love us?

Ahmad   You and Khalil?

Samar   Yes.

Ahmad   Of course I do. You're all I have.

Samar   He's growing up.

Ahmad   Oh . . . He'll be a man soon.

Samar   Where did he get that habit from?

Ahmad   What habit?

Samar   The way he blows on his fingers when he's talking.

Ahmad   He's always picking up funny habits.

Samar   No one in my family has ever done that. None of them have ever blown on their fingers when they're talking. They're good speakers. If they use their hands for anything, it's for pointing at people to threaten them.

Ahmad   He picks these habits up from time to time, then they go away again.

Samar   Maybe we should tie his hands until he forgets how to do it.

They look at each other then both laugh. Long Pause.

Samar   We can be happy again.

Ahmad   We are happy.

Samar   Then why do you want to blow up a restaurant?

Long Pause.

I heard you talking with your friend.

Ahmad   What did you hear?

Samar   That you want to scare them. Are you going to die?

Ahmad   . . .

Samar   You're going to blow yourself up?

Ahmad   No, I'm not going to blow myself up.

Samar   Blow yourself into 20,000 pieces? So they can pick you up, piece by piece?

Ahmad   I'm not going to blow myself up. Where would I blow myself up?

Samar   So are you the one making the bomb? Do you know how to make a bomb? Where did you learn how to make a bomb?

Ahmad   No, I'm not going to make a bomb. We're not going to blow anything up.

Samar   I heard you saying you're going to call and threaten them.

Ahmad   There is no bomb. It's all made up.

Samar   Is there a bomb or not?

Ahmad   There's no bomb.

Samar   There's no bomb?

Ahmad   There's no bomb.

Samar   So the restaurant won't be blown up?

Ahmad   It won't be blown up.

Samar   No one's going to die?

Ahmad   No one's going to die.

Samar   So why?

Ahmad   So they get scared.

Samar   Scared?

Ahmad   Yes, scared. So they know what it feels like to be scared, so they know they should always be scared.

Samar   Where did you get the restaurant's number?

Ahmad   I got it.

Samar   How did you get it?

Ahmad   From a friend who used to work there.

Samar   Work as what?

Ahmad   He used to work there. He used to wash dishes.

Samar   What if they actually believe there's a bomb?

Ahmad   They have to believe there's a bomb!

Samar   But I thought there was no bomb.

Ahmad   They have to think there's a bomb. That's the whole point. They get scared, and they run away, and they get completely confused. And then they start getting scared just thinking about going out or going to a bar or going to a café, or going –

Samar   Why?!

Ahmad   Because we don't have tanks, and we don't have weapons, and we don't have planes, and we don't have anything. The only thing we can do is make them scared.

Samar   You're just going to call a restaurant and tell them there's a bomb when there isn't? Risk our lives for that?

Ahmad   It's just a threat. To scare them a bit. so they understand what it's like to be crammed into our houses waiting to be blown up. It's been weeks already and God knows how long it will last. They're killing us like flies. They've destroyed our city. I went up on the roof. You can't recognise it anymore . . . It'll never be the same again. They've ruined everything. Have you seen what's happening? Have you seen on TV? Through the windows? Have you been able to sleep? There's nothing left of it. When was the last time you slept? When Khalil asks questions, I don't know what to say. I don't know what to tell him, what to teach him. And right now right now right now when we're dying, when they're killing us just because they can, when we're silent in front of our kids' questions, they're on top of a hill watching the planes bombing us and cheering. They're cheering. An hour away from here they're living. They're going on with their lives, they're not scared, they think they think they think they can do anything and nothing will happen to them. They're happy. They can put their children to bed and know they'll find them there in the morning. They can send their kids to school and know they won't have to come and pick them up in pieces. They think they can do whatever they want, and we'll forget. No no no no no, we won't forget. No I'm not going to forget, and you're not going to forget and Khalil won't forget, no, Khalil won't forget. You can forget for a while, yes, for a while when they're busy with life. But it'll always come back, haunt us. We can make them scared, make them terrified, make them look over their shoulders when they're out, when they're on the bus, when they're having a night out, when they're on the beach, when they're just walking about. Now just think – when I call the bar and they all get up and run about like they've lost their minds. Just think of them running out into the street in their nice dresses and their high heels and their fancy suits, the girls with make-up running down their faces because they're scared. Then they'll remember what's happening here, what's happening an hour away. Then they'll think of us. Maybe they'll know? Maybe they'll stop? Maybe something buried deep inside them will wake up.

Samar   You're not going to do this.

Ahmad   I already have.

Long Pause.

Samar   What if they tracked the call?

Ahmad   I used a different number.

Samar   Different number? You think they can't work it out? They know everything. They know what we eat and where we sleep. They know everything about us.

Ahmad   That's enough. I've had enough.

Samar   I'm taking Khalil and I'm leaving.

Ahmad   No. We can't leave the building . . . This is the safest place to be. We're not changing anything. We'll get sick in the shelter. Everyone gets sick there.

Samar   I'm not staying here, it's too dangerous now. They'll know. I'll tell the neighbours they have to leave.

Scene Fifteen

Lubna   Open the door.

Khalil   Count to a hundred.

Lubna   Open the door. You're crazy. Open the door.

Khalil   Count backwards to a hundred.

Lubna   Crazy. Craaaaazy.

Khalil   Don't be like my dad.

Lubna for me.   Open the door. My mum'll be coming out to look

Khalil   Stand on one leg.

Lubna   OK, if you open the door, I'll stand on one leg.

Khalil   And count backwards?

Lubna   OK, I'll count backwards and stand on one leg.

Khalil   Before I open.

Lubna   No. I have to be inside.

Khalil   Come on. I can't hear you.

Lubna   I can't stay outside. I could die.

Khalil   No one dies except liars.

Lubna   If you open the door I'll teach you dabkeh.

Khalil   Really?

Lubna   Yes. I'll teach you all the moves.

Khalil   And you'll hold my hand?

Lubna   I'll hold your hand.

Khalil   Even if I haven't washed?

Lubna   Yes. Just open up now, let me in.

Khalil   What if you're lying to me . . .

Lubna   I'm not lying.

Khalil   I don't believe you.

Lubna   If I die, my dad will shoot you.

Khalil   How will he shoot me?

Lubna   He'll shoot you in the head.

Khalil   Does your dad have a gun?

Lubna   He'll buy one.

Khalil   From where?

Lubna   From the police.

Khalil   If your dad shoots me, my mum'll shoot him.

Lubna   If your mum shoots him, my mum'll shoot
your mum.

Khalil   Then my dad'll shoot your mum.

Lubna   Your dad can't shoot.

Khalil   Why?

Lubna   Because he's a wimp.

Khalil   My dad's not a wimp.

Lubna   Everyone knows he's a wimp.

Khalil   Don't talk like that.

Lubna   Ask him and he'll tell you.

Khalil   My dad's strong. I'm scared of him.

He opens the door. She comes in and pushes him.

Lubna   Idiot.

Khalil   How do you know my dad's a wimp?

Lubna   There are a lot of things that I know and you don't.

Khalil   How come?

Lubna   Because Lubna in the sky tells me everything.

Khalil   She talks to you?

Lubna   Yes. She even takes me to the sky at night so I can sleep

Khalil   Liar.

Lubna   Last night she came down and flew me to the sky.

Khalil   What did you do?

Lubna   We watched cartoons and then we played thieves and soldiers and then we slept.

Khalil   That's not fun . . . That's what we do at school. We play thieves and soldiers all the time at school . . .

Lubna   Yes but it's different when we play it in the sky . . . because there are chocolates everywhere, so you're running and trying to catch each other but when you're tired you can stop and pick a chocolate up from the ground or whisper 'juice' and then juice appears in front of you.

Khalil   Wow.

Lubna   I don't like Lubna in the sky . . . She's stupid

Khalil   Doesn't she know how to play thieves and soldiers?

Lubna   No . . . And she doesn't really look like me. But she knows everything, everything we do.

Khalil   Really?

Lubna   Yes she knows all the secrets

Khalil   Does she know my secrets?

Lubna   Yes and she told me everything

Khalil   Tell me.

Lubna   I don't want to tell you because if I tell you they won't be secrets anymore.

Khalil   Did she tell you we're leaving?

Lubna   Who's leaving?

Khalil   Me and Mum, we're going to the school.

Lubna   When?

Khalil   Today.

Lubna   But tomorrow's Eid.

Khalil   I know.

Lubna   Are you telling the truth?

Khalil   Yes. She's getting ready, Dad wants to stay but Mum says she doesn't.

Lubna   OK.

Khalil   Is Lubna in the sky your new friend?

Lubna   No.

Khalil   Are you going to play with her on Eid?

Lubna   No.

Khalil   Will you come to the playground tomorrow?

Lubna   . . .

Khalil   It's Eid . . . we can play together.

She climbs the stairs.

OK?

OK?

OK?

She looks back at him and nods. She runs upstairs.

Scene Sixteen

Lubna   Where's Mum?

Khalid   Mum?

Lubna   Isn't she at home?

Khalid   She went out for a little walk.

Lubna   She left the building?

Khalid   Just now. She'll be back in a minute.

Lubna   Did she take the bag?

Khalid   The bag? Which bag? Oh! The bag with the things in it. No. What an idea! Of course she didn't take the bag.

Lubna   Why did you let her leave?

Khalid   I didn't let her . . . She left without telling me. I didn't notice.

Lubna   She didn't tell anyone?

Khalid   No.

Lubna   She's just disappeared?

Khalid   No, she –

Lubna   Will she find her way back?

Khalid   Of course she will.

Lubna   I told you she'd leave.

Khalid   She just went out to get some candles from the shop. We've run out.

Pause.

Lubna   Why were you on the balcony?

Khalid   Just getting some fresh air.

Lubna   But you said I wasn't allowed to go out on the balcony because it doesn't have railings.

Khalid   Yes, but –

Lubna   You're scared she won't know her way back.

Khalid   I told you she's coming back.

Pause.

Lubna   I know you've been hiding things from me.

Khalid   What things?

Lubna   You don't want to tell me because you think I'm little.

Khalid   I know you're not little. That's why I don't hide anything from you. Everything I tell you is true.

Lubna   There are things you don't tell me.

Khalid   There are some things you need to be a little bit older to know.

Lubna   I'm not little anymore.

Khalid   I know you're not little.

You can write poetry –

Lubna   Songs.

Khalid   Songs. You're really not little anymore.

Lubna   Not just that.

Pause.

Blood comes out of me.

Khalid   Blood?

Lubna   Mum told me not to tell you because you faint when you see blood, but blood comes out of me.

Khalid   Since when?

Lubna   Two days ago.

Khalid   Really?

Lubna   Do you actually faint?

Khalid   No, of course not . . .

Lubna   Me neither. Sometimes I put my fingers down there and see it on my fingers and I don't faint.

Khalid   Right . . . You're right . . . You really have grown up . . . You've grown up and you're not afraid of blood.

Lubna   That's why you have to start telling me things.

Khalid   Tell me what you want to know.

Lubna   I know you don't want to tell me that Mum's going crazy.

Khalid   Oh . . . That's what you think I'm hiding from you?

Lubna   But it's OK. I'll forgive you because I've been hiding things from you too.

Khalid   What have you been hiding from me?

Lubna   I didn't want to tell you because I didn't want you to get scared and upset.

Khalid   What?

Lubna   But I've got to tell you because you've got to know because we've got to look after Mum and we can't let her out.

Khalid   What is it? Tell me.

Lubna   You know the planes in the sky.

Khalid   Yes.

Lubna   They're not ambulance planes. They're planes which bomb people.

Khalid   . . .

Lubna   And the sounds we hear. It's not fireworks. It's bombs. And lots of people are dying and having their legs cut off.

Khalid   Who told you that?

Lubna   I know . . . Everyone knows apart from you, Dad.
Because you haven't left the house since Ali died.

Khalid   You mustn't talk like this.

Lubna   Why not?

Khalid   Because Mum will come back now and we can't talk
about this stuff in front of her . . . We've got to always talk
about nice things.

Lubna   Because she's scared.

Khalid   Because she's scared and we've got to help her . . .
And we can't think about those things because if we think
about them then we might get like she is too.

Lubna   I don't think about them all the time. Just
sometimes before I go to sleep.

Khalid   You should think about something else.

Lubna   Like what?

Khalid   Think about the Lubna in the sky. And the
magic tape.

Lubna   The magic tape isn't really magic. We can get
bombed and die too.

Khalid   But –

Lubna   And now there'll be no one left in the building
apart from us. Because the neighbours upstairs are leaving.

Khalid   They're leaving?!

Lubna   Yes, Khalil and his mum are leaving.

Khalid   Where are they going?

Lubna   To a shelter.

Khalid   Do you want us to leave?

Pause.

Lubna   Is Lubna in the sky real?

Khalid   Of course she's real.

Pause.

Lubna   It's Eid tomorrow and it'll all stop, won't it? We don't have to leave.

Khalid   Yes, that's right. It's Eid tomorrow and it'll all stop. It's Eid tomorrow and it'll all stop. It's Eid tomorrow and it'll all stop.

Scene Seventeen

Nahla   Why do you dream about my son?

Samar   I don't know, maybe –

Nahla   Don't you have other things to dream about?

Samar   . . .

Nahla   Why don't you dream about your son, your husband, your family? You can dream about me, or my husband, why does it have to be my little angel?

Samar   No one chooses their dreams . . .

Nahla   He's *my* Ali . . . I didn't carry him inside me for nine months and bring him up so that when he died a stranger could come along and dream about him every night.

Samar   I understand it must be difficult.

Nahla   You know I had him inside me for nine months.

Samar   Of course.

Nahla   Even if I had him for seven months, it doesn't make me less of a mother than anyone else. It doesn't mean it's OK for someone else to dream about him.

Samar   I think I know now why he visits me.

Nahla   He has a message.

Samar   Yes.

Nahla   If he has a message he should come straight to me. I haven't completely lost it. I can understand a message.

Samar   It's an important message; you have to listen to me.

Nahla   I'm not going to hear another dream about my son. I'm the one who went to his grave, collected what's left with my bare hands and carried it all the way back here. I'm the one who should be dreaming about him.

Samar   Maybe it's because you haven't been sleeping.

Nahla   I sleep sometimes. He doesn't come . . . He's happy without me now, he doesn't miss me anymore . . . He thinks he's all grown up and doesn't need his mother . . . You tell him children in the sky stay children. Tell him he'll never grow up.

Samar   Listen to me!

Nahla   I don't want to listen. And I don't want you to dream about him . . . Tell him never to come again. Be horrible. Scare him off.

Samar   He says it's safer to leave the building . . . That's all he said, he –

Nahla   We're not leaving the building. It's Eid tomorrow. I made his cake. I don't want to hear anything about it

Samar   We should leave as soon as possible.

Nahla   If he wants to tell me anything, he comes straight to me. I'm angry with him now, leaving me all alone and wandering around in strangers' dreams.

She tears up his photo.

Scene Eighteen

Ahmad *is sitting.* **Khalil** *doesn't want to leave.*

Samar   The man with three arms didn't know what to do with his life. His mother said you should become a typist, you'll be the fastest. His friends said you should join the army, you'll be firing three guns at the same time and you'll be a hero. The little girl who lives in his building and always eats ice cream said you should sell balloons at the zoo – you could carry the balloons with two hands and use the third to pat the children on their shoulders. His wife said you should become a gardener, you'll plant three trees every minute and the town will look better. His son said you should be a fireman – you could quickly put out all the fires that keep happening and no one would die. The man with the three arms spent long hours sitting on his front doorstep thinking about all the great things he could do with his three arms. One day when he was sitting there, something that turned out to be a dead bird fell from the sky and broke his third arm. His third arm flew away from him and fell on the head of the girl who always eats ice cream and killed her immediately. The man was horrified. He ran down the stairs to help the little girl and get his third arm back but when he got there, the little girl was standing and smiling with a third arm that came out of her chest. The girl said: 'Now I'm the girl with three arms.' From then on she always walked around the neighbourhood eating three ice creams at the same time.

Did you like the story?

Khalil *nods.*

Samar   Ready?

Khalil *nods.*

Samar   Let's go.

They leave.

Scene Nineteen

Khalid   Beautiful day, isn't it?

Ahmad   Lovely.

Khalid   Not too hot.

Ahmad   It's lovely.

Khalid   Not a cloud in the sky

Ahmad   Khalil was born in the spring.

Khalid   Was he?

Ahmad   Well he wasn't actually born in spring. It felt like it was spring. The weather was like this

Khalid   He loved it when it was like this.

Ahmad   It's lovely.

Khalid   Glorious.

Ahmad   So clear.

Khalid   He loved it when it was clear.

Ahmad   Sure he did.

Khalid   He never said it. But I knew.

Ahmad   It's absolutely lovely.

Khalid   I was telling my wife how lovely it was.

Ahmad   I'm really happy.

Khalid   I'm happy too.

Ahmad   Khalil would be happy.

Khalid   Ali would have been happy.

Pause.

Khalid *walks around,* **Ahmad** *is still looking out of the window.* **Khalid** *sits down.*

Khalid   I forgot his name. I forgot my baby boy's name. I forgot his name. I have to go to his grave to remember his name. To read his name on the gravestone. I have to go to the cemetery. I have to pretend there is a cemetery. I have to pretend that I lost my baby child. I have to pretend that I forgot my baby boy's name. I have to pretend that I'm not lying on the floor and watching the sky. I have to pretend that the screams I'm hearing come from the TV. I have to pretend that his grave is as small as a pebble. I have to pretend they didn't put his body in a plastic bag. I have to pretend to watch them collecting the bits of his body on the TV. I have to pretend that the children who are running are chasing a clown. I have to sew up his wounds with my bare hands. I forgot my baby boy's name.

He gets out a pistol and tries to shoot himself. He can't do it. Finally he throws the pistol on the floor and starts crying, **Ahmad** *hugs him. The two men cry.*

Scene Twenty

Some stones from **Ali**'s *destroyed grave on the ground.* **Lubna** *is playing with them and arranging them to look like a grave.* **Nahla** *comes in.*

Lubna   Do you like it?

Nahla   Yes.

Lubna   I've rebuilt his grave, it's not destroyed anymore . . .

Nahla   Yes.

Lubna   Now you don't have to go to the graveyard to visit him.

Nahla   No we don't.

Lubna   We can have a picnic and bring food like we used to and sit near his grave and talk to him.

Nahla   Do you think he can hear us?

Lubna   Yes! Always. Shall I bring him the Eid cakes?

Nahla   Yes, bring them . . .

Lubna   We can have Eid together . . .

Nahla   I bought you Eid clothes.

Lubna   When?

Nahla   When I went out.

Lubna   Really?

Nahla   I bought you that bag you like.

Lubna   Show me.

Nahla   You like them?

Lubna   I don't deserve them.

Nahla   Why not?

Lubna   Because I broke Ali's photo.

Nahla   It's fine, it wasn't on purpose.

Lubna   No, it was. I broke it.

Nahla   Why?

Lubna   I was jealous.

Nahla   You were jealous of Ali?

Lubna   Because you love him more than me, but now I don't care. You can love him more.

Nahla   I don't love him more. How did you get that into your head?

Lubna   You always talk about him.

Nahla   Because I miss him. Go on, take your Eid clothes. Don't you like them?

Lubna   I love them! I can't wait to wear them tomorrow.

Nahla   Tomorrow you'll go out and play with Khalil and your friends on the beach and you'll be wearing the nicest clothes of all of them . . .

Lubna   Thank you, Mum.

Nahla   Everyone will be jealous of your bag . . . Everyone will want a bag like yours.

Lubna   It's so nice I'm going to take it everywhere . . .

Nahla   And when they ask you who got you this bag . . . you will say my mum . . . my mum got me this bag.

Lubna   I love you, Mum!

Nahla   And they'll be jealous and everyone will want a mum like yours, won't they?

Lubna   Yes, Mum . . . (*Pause.*) I don't think I'm going out tomorrow.

Nahla   Why not?

Lubna   Because I want to stay with you.

Nahla   No, you have to go and play . . . Tomorrow everything will be OK.

Lubna   But what if you leave the house?

Nahla   Don't worry, I won't leave the house.

Lubna   Are you sure?

Nahla   Yes I'll stay with Ali.

Lubna   Promise?

Nahla   I promise!

Lubna   Happy Eid, Mum!

Nahla   Happy Eid . . . Happy Eid . . . Happy Eid.

Scene Twenty-One

A playground. **Lubna** *and* **Khalil** *are playing. They are running and screaming and jumping around. They are happy. They are wearing special clothes for Eid. They play for a while, then suddenly we hear an explosion. He dies. She, dressed in her Eid clothes, tells a story as if it's twenty years later.*

Lubna   I want to tell you a story. It's actually a poem I tried to write twenty years ago. The poem is about a little boy and a little girl. One day, someone said to the little girl, 'Look, can you see that point where the sky meets the sea. That's where heaven is.' And the little girl loved heaven because it was a really beautiful place and no bad people lived there. And whenever her father told her, 'Ohhhh but you still have a really, really, really long time until you die,' she felt a little bit sad. Because she didn't want to wait a really, really, really long time, because her brother was there and he was playing on his own. So every night she asked God to take her to heaven as soon as possible, and every night she imagined how the angels would come down and fly her up to the sky. And one day the little girl met a little boy, and she said to the little boy, 'Look, can you see that point in the distance where the sky meets the sea. That's where the world ends and heaven starts.' And before she could tell him heaven was a really beautiful place and there were no bad people there, the little boy got angry and said, 'No, that's not true, there's nothing there, and there are bad people everywhere.' The little girl was a bit upset because the little boy didn't believe her, but then she thought he doesn't know what she knows and maybe it's because he's a bit strange and he blows on his fingers when he talks. So the little girl didn't talk to him about heaven again. And one day the little girl and the little boy were playing and the little boy was wearing his flashing trainers and red lights flashed when he ran and the little girl was so happy. Then, suddenly, something happened. The little girl doesn't remember exactly what happened but when she opened her eyes the little boy wasn't moving, and he wasn't blowing on his fingers, and he wasn't screaming.

Nothing was moving except for the flashing red lights in his trainers. The little girl closed her eyes and tried to think of that point where the sky meets the sea. But as soon as she closed her eyes she saw the little boy not moving again. The little girl started walking about looking for someone but there were other little children on the ground and none of them were moving. And she thought maybe the angels will come down now and fly him up to the sky. Then she noticed that the boy's little hand, the hand he blew on when he was speaking, wasn't there. And she didn't want him to be the only boy in the sky without a hand. So she started rushing to find it before the angels came, then the parents of the children arrived. They started hugging them, hugging them really tight, as if they didn't want anyone to take them away. The little girl got scared. She wanted to run far away and hide in a place where she wouldn't hear the parents screaming. She put her hands over her ears and closed her eyes. But as soon as she shut her eyes she saw the boy. She saw him not blowing on his fingers and not running in his flashing trainers. Lying there, not moving, missing a hand. The girl opened her eyes and started crying and the boy's mother was crying and everyone was hugging the boy's mother and telling her not to worry, that he's happy now, in the sky, happy with God. But the girl thought he's not in the sky, and he's not happy. He's right there, in front of her. She can see him whenever she shuts her eyes. The girl tried to explain to someone that the boy was still there. And the angels hadn't come to fly him up to the sky. But everyone was busy telling the boy's mother how happy he was in the sky and no one would listen to the girl. So the girl decided to keep it secret, and she started sleeping with her eyes open every night so she wouldn't see the little boy. And she started to get black bags under her eyes. And the girl still sleeps with her eyes open, and whenever she sees on TV that someone's died she knows that there's another person sleeping with their eyes open. And the girl knows that one day there will be lots and lots of people who sleep with their eyes open and they will know each other from the black bags under their eyes.

I

9 781474 244503